Dwayne "The Rock" Johnson

In His Own Words

Dwayne "The Rock" Johnson

In His Own Words

EDITED BY
Kelsey Dame
and Eva Lopez

A B2 BOOK
AGATE
CHICAGO

Printed in United States of America

First printing: February 2025

Library of Congress Cataloging-in-Publication Data

Names: | Dame, Kelsey, editor. | Lopez, Eva, editor.
Title: Dwayne "The Rock" Johnson : in his own words / edited by Kelsey Dame and Eva Lopez.
Description: Chicago : Agate, [2025] | Series: In their own words | "A B2 Book." |
Identifiers: LCCN 2024039036 (print) | LCCN 2024039037 (ebook) | ISBN 9781572843486 (paperback) | ISBN 9781572848931 (ebook)
Subjects: LCSH: Johnson, Dwayne, 1972- | Johnson, Dwayne, 1972---Quotations. | Wrestlers--United States--Quotations. | Actors--United States--Quotations.
Classification: LCC GV1196.J64 A25 2025 (print) | LCC GV1196.J64 (ebook) | DDC 796.812092 [B]--dc23/eng/20241011
LC record available at https://lccn.loc.gov/2024039036
LC ebook record available at https://lccn.loc.gov/2024039037

10 9 8 7 6 5 4 3 2 1 25 26 27 28 29

B2 Books is an imprint of Agate Publishing. Agate books are available in bulk at discount prices. For more information, go to agatepublishing.com.

Can we cuss on this thing? Yeah, we can cuss.
Good. Fuck yeah.

—The Rock YouTube channel,
October 28, 2016

I owe that name everything. Without that name there'd be no wrestling career. There'd be no Hollywood career.

—Associated Press, January 23, 2024

Contents

Introduction

There are few celebrities more recognizable than Dwayne "The Rock" Johnson. To some, he's the punk kid from Hawaii who hustled tourists and got arrested, or a failed professional football player. To others, he's Rocky Maivia, the up-and-coming wrestler, or The People's Champion, the World Wrestling Entertainment (WWE) poster boy. Many know him best as the Tooth Fairy, Luke Hobbs, or Dr. Smolder Bravestone from Hollywood, a potential politician, or the businessman behind an entertainment production company, a tasty tequila, and the XFL (now UFL) football league. Dwayne Johnson's story is one of transformation and hard work, beginning at the edge of poverty and climbing to a level of stardom and success spanning industries and decades that only an elite few have experienced.

Johnson's life has been heavily influenced by his early years. His father, Rocky Johnson, believed in tough love and hard work. He was a professional wrestler in an era when performers were expected to project the image of success but were paid poorly. His mother, Ata Maivia, offered unconditional love and a sense of legacy. She came from a storied Samoan wrestling family: Her mother, Lia Maivia, was one of the first female wrestling promoters and was married to "High Chief" Peter Maivia, also of wrestling fame.

Dwayne Johnson's childhood was unstable. The family moved frequently because of his father's wrestling career, and they faced financial hardship and uncertainty. This exposed Johnson to the unpredictable nature of the entertainment industry, and it strained his relationship with his father. Johnson often cites the moment his family was evicted from their home in Hawaii as a turning point—he never wanted to feel that low or helpless again. As a teenager, Johnson's frustration with his upbringing turned into anger and rebellion. He was suspended from school twice and arrested multiple times for theft, fighting, and check fraud.

Johnson's turnaround came through sports. In 11th grade, Johnson was caught using the faculty bathroom by a teacher named Jody Cwik. When reprimanded, Johnson initially talked back, but he later apologized. Cwik shook Johnson's hand and told him he should join the football team. Cwik became a mentor to Johnson, and, with Cwik's guidance, Johnson earned a football scholarship at the University of Miami.

In 1991, Johnson's college team won the national championship. Johnson hoped football would be his ticket out of poverty and joined the Canadian Football League after being skipped over by the NFL. But after a series of injuries, Johnson became the 54th player on a roster of 53. He was cut from the team and, with around $7 to his name, went back to live with his parents.

After the football false start, Johnson found his home in local wrestling rings earning $40 a day. It didn't take long for Johnson's talents as a wrestler and a performer to be discovered, and he quickly followed in the footsteps of his father and maternal grandfather. Entering the world of professional wrestling under the moniker "The Rock," Johnson became a sensation in the World Wrestling Federation (WWF, now

WWE) nearly overnight. His charisma, catchphrases, and larger-than-life persona made him one of the most popular wrestlers of all time. He won numerous championships, became a central figure in the organization's Attitude Era, and helped bring professional wrestling into mainstream culture.

However, Johnson's ambitions extended beyond wrestling. In the early 2000s, he took his talents to Hollywood. In his role as the Scorpion King in *The Mummy Returns* and *The Scorpion King,* he belied skeptics and was lauded by critics. Further roles proved he wasn't just an action star but could also shine in comedies, dramas, and musicals. Johnson charmed audiences with his humor and physical presence and became one of the highest-grossing actors in Hollywood.

In recent years, Johnson has branched out into entrepreneurial efforts. His company, Seven Bucks Productions (named for his net worth after his CFL flameout), has produced most of his movies since 2017. He's also partnered with sportswear brands, developed a personal hygiene brand and an energy drink, and is the co-owner of the United Football League. And Johnson has returned to the WWE to face off against John Cena as well as other iconic foes.

In his personal life, Johnson has experienced both joy and heartbreak. His marriage to Dany Garcia ended in divorce, though they remain friendly co-parents to their daughter, and Garcia still oversees and manages Johnson's business portfolio. He later married Lauren Hashian, with whom he has two daughters. Johnson has expressed regret about not being present for his eldest daughter. Work kept him away from his family, just as his own father's work had. Johnson is determined to make sure that doesn't happen again, and has turned down Hollywood roles, wrestling contracts, and even presidential campaigns to ensure he makes time for his younger children.

Through everything, Johnson has carried three core tenets: maintaining good physical and mental health, working hard, and honoring his roots. It's difficult to have a physique like Johnson's without a dedication to healthy eating and exercise—but Johnson focuses on fostering discipline, resilience, and positivity over physical gains. He has also been open about his struggles with depression and has endeavored to destigmatize mental health conditions by speaking about his own experiences. Johnson's Samoan roots are also a significant part of his identity. His tattoos have Polynesian tribal origins, and he often speaks about the importance of *mana*, a supernatural power or energy.

At every obstacle, Johnson has met the challenge and overcome it. He is called "one of Hollywood's busiest men" and always aims to be the hardest worker in the room, willing to put in the time and the energy to do right by himself, his family, and his fans. From his tumultuous upbringing to his rise in football, wrestling, and Hollywood, he has continually reinvented himself, driven by a desire to achieve and inspire. His journey underscores the power of perseverance and the impact of embracing one's heritage, family, and personal challenges. Johnson's ability to turn adversity into opportunity and his unwavering work ethic serve as a testament to his extraordinary life.

Part I

PART ONE: EARLY LIFE

Family Turmoil

My parents met when my dad's tag team partner was my grandfather, Peter Maivia. They kept their relationship a secret...until they got caught & were forbid to see each other. BUT my mom had a solve. She got pregnant. I was born. The rest is history.

—Twitter, April 26, 2022

I grew up an only child. Got a lot of love. It's that mama love—mama's boy. Love that I was so blessed to get. And that tough love from my dad, which I was so blessed to get.

—*Oprah's Master Class*, July 17, 2018

He showed love through discipline. His love was, "Come here and kiss me on the cheek. I'm going to work."

—*WSJ Magazine*, December 3, 2019

At a very early age, from my mom and my dad, it was always, "What you are is perfect, and what you are is cool."

—*What Now? with Trevor Noah*, November 9, 2023

So, BE PROUD of everything that you are. So, out of the gates, it was always be proud.

—***What Now? with Trevor Noah,*** **November 9, 2023**

I WAS ALWAYS changing schools . . . starting over again and again as we moved with my dad around the country. I didn't know anything else and it was tough.

—***British GQ,*** **November 15, 2016**

WHEN I WAS a little punk kid living in Hawaii, my grandfather (wrestler, High Chief Peter Maivia) used to promote tiny wrestling shows on this base every week and would draw a few hundred people at best. Never made any money, we lived paycheck to paycheck, but he loved supporting the military and would always love to come "work out with da boys" on the base before every wrestling show.

—Instagram, May 19, 2018

A WRESTLER'S LIFE was like a circus - we moved from state to state every year or so. Back when pro wrestling was a wild (and often violent) subculture of entertainment.

—Twitter, December 23, 2019

OH, YES, WE are showing the truth of that generation, of the '70s and '80s. Those wrestling stars were adored and they were celebrated. They would wrestle in 5,000-seat arenas or in high-school gyms. And when they left, they always left in a Cadillac or a Lincoln. Always. Everyone. Wherever they would park, you would see a fleet of Caddies and Lincolns. Because that was working the gimmick. And it was important that fans saw them getting into an expensive car. But then when you go down the road, to where they lived, in many cases it was small apartments, like we did.

***—New York Times,* February 15, 2021**

Dreams ain't just for dreamers.

When I was an 11yr old punk kid, I'd go into NYC with my old man and we'd always walk Times Square around 1am for our "midnight snack" of burgers and fries.

I'd look up at all the bright lights and billboards and just be in a state of awe and dreaming.

—Instagram, November 13, 2017

So, twelve years old, in Hawaii, my dad finally said, "Alright you can go to the gym with me." It was a Saturday, so I was really pumped to go to the gym with my dad. I was twelve, and before we walked in, he said, "Listen, you're gonna work your ass off. I don't want any bullshit."

—The Rock YouTube channel, March 29, 2020

"Here's a lesson for you," he said. "Don't worry about other people looking at you and don't ego train, don't ever train for your ego, doesn't matter. Who gives a shit who's watching you, you train for the results and you train with weight you can control."

—The Rock YouTube channel, March 29, 2020

My old man would tell me bedtime stories about John Henry, and he'd always sing me, "Big John" to put me to sleep. Then of course the next day, he'd take me down to the gym and beat my ass on the wrestling mats.

—Instagram, October 10, 2018

When I was growing up there wasn't a real consistency in terms of home life.

—The Rock YouTube channel, February 16, 2021

Like all kids, my parents marriage had an effect on me. When they struggled, I struggled too.

—Twitter, October 9, 2022

We never lived in a house, it was always apartments and mobile homes, so, there was really no anchoring in. . . . It was just my life.

—*Sunday Sitdown*, May 2, 2021

When we were evicted off the island in Honolulu, Hawaii, . . . I told myself then when I was fourteen, "I need to buy my mom a house."

—*Jimmy Kimmel Live*, July 21, 2022

WE CAME HOME, and we were evicted. There was an eviction on the door with a padlock. And it was me and my mom and I'll never forget, I looked at her and she started crying, and at that point we had hit an all-time low. I told myself I was going to do everything I could possibly do to make sure we were never evicted again.

—*Oprah's Master Class*, July 17, 2018

WHEN I FIRST met Milton I was a kid, probably five, six years old, and for me it was just another buddy. Milton was one of the ones who showed me how to start working out. We wound up moving in with the Rosens, and then I shared a bedroom with Milton and that started to solidify our friendship and our brotherhood and we got extremely close.

—on Special Olympics athlete Milton Rosen, The Rock YouTube channel, April 10, 2019

My childhood was wild, in that I grew up in the world of professional wrestling.

—***Sunday Sitdown,*** **May 2, 2021**

Up until I was sixteen years old, we lived on the road, and I spent a lot of my time growing up in the back seat of a car.

—*CBS Sunday Morning*, December 5, 2022

It was this unique upbringing that I had that converged and intersected with all these amazing heroes of mine in the world of pro wrestling, but then, you know, there's a lot of life lessons that I didn't know I was being taught back then.

—*Sunday Sitdown*, May 2, 2021

Now while other kids were playing with G.I. Joe, I was playing with Andre the Giant. And while other grandmothers were knitting blankets, my badass grandma ran the family wrestling business.

—The Rock YouTube channel, March 14, 2022

EVERY THANKSGIVING I gotta take a moment to remember exactly 27 years ago on Thanksgiving while living in Tampa, Fl we were so piss broke, that we couldn't even afford to buy a turkey, so we were praying someone would invite us over for Thanksgiving.

. . . Remembering shit like this helps me live a better and more grateful life.

—Instagram, November 23, 2018

PART ONE: EARLY LIFE

Bad Kid

I DIDN'T LIKE my parents fighting, my dad being on the road, not making much money. It was tough . . . and I was getting into a lot of fights.

—*British GQ*, November 15, 2016

I HAD A hard time staying on the right track and had a hard time staying in school and had a lot of arrests doing things I shouldn't be doing.

—*Variety*, December 13, 2017

AT FOURTEEN YEARS old, yes I was out here, I was busting my ass, I was working as hard as I possibly could in the weight room . . . but at the same time I struggled to stay on the right path.

—The Rock YouTube channel, February 15, 2021

EVERY DAY I used to stop here at this 7/11 and steal a king-sized Snickers bar because I couldn't afford to buy one. That was my pre-workout food. I did that almost a year every day. I had to come back and buy every Snickers bar on those shelves.

—TikTok, November 28, 2022

I ALSO USED to hustle the gym front desk employee who would always tell me I was months behind on my membership dues. I was broke as fuck but would always say "absolutely brothaaa, next week I'll bring you tha cash" then I'd throw him a 👍 with a smile and a wink.

The next week would come, I'd still be broke and looking for another way to hustle my way into the gym.

—Instagram, May 27, 2018

At 10, I was rambunctious as all hell, girl crazy & loved pro wrestling - especially the blood. But at the core I was a sweet, complicated cub who just needed guidance.

—Twitter, September 30, 2020

I PILE DRIVED a kid in elementary.

KO'd a kid in high school.

Got suspended both times.

I was wrong.

But back in the 80s I was taught by my dad and all the wrestlers to always "protect the business." It's what we we did.

—Twitter, February 23, 2021

I WOULD STEAL food. I would steal steak and cookies, or anything I could get my hands on. And that's how we would eat every day.

—*Oprah's Master Class*, July 17, 2018

#FLASHBACKFRIDAY TO THAT special time when I was a 15yr old punk kid, 6'4, barely 200lbs, creepy mustache and forced to leave Hawai'i to live in Nashville, TN - where I just enrolled in a new high school - and EVERYONE (students and teachers) treated me like I had the plague and stayed away because they were all convinced I was an undercover cop.

—Instagram, October 18, 2019

I WAS ARRESTED multiple times for fighting.... I was running around with the wrong people, making the wrong decisions.... I didn't come from a broken home. My mom loved me. Still to this day, she's my biggest fan. And my dad too, but I wasn't listening to them. I thought I knew everything.

—*East Bay Times*, September 15, 2006

I WAS NEVER disrespectful to adults. . . . In the Samoan culture, that is a big no-no. . . . I would be getting into fights all the time at school, but all the teachers were saying: "He's such a good kid, a pleasure to have in class."

—*British GQ*, November 15, 2016

I WAS SUSPENDED for knocking a kid out who was talking shit AND got arrested (again) for theft. After seeing how much pain I was causing my mom at an already difficult time in our lives (pay check to pay check), I decided this was my last arrest and I needed to straighten my shit out - because I didn't want to be a source of disappointment anymore for my mom.

—Instagram, March 22, 2021

IT TURNED OUT he was the teacher that looked after all the tough kids, the troublemakers. So already he is expecting the worst. Anyway I talked to him, apologised, explained how sorry I was for my behaviour and offered to shake his hand. He took my hand, held onto it and said, "Thank you. I want you to play football for me." . . . His name was Jody Cwik and he turned my life around.

—on talking back to a teacher after using the teachers' bathroom, *British GQ*, November 15, 2016

[BEFORE] ANYTHING BIG that would happen, I would always take a moment and I'd just remind myself: I was evicted when I was fourteen, we were kicked off the island, we couldn't live in Hawaii, we had no place to live, a lot of shit happened then when I moved to Nashville, I was arrested multiple times by the time I was sixteen years old. . . . It allows me then to be present in the moment and understand holy shit, the stuff I have around me right now, this is the shit that I dreamed of when I was a kid, I am here.

— The Rock YouTube channel, May 15, 2018

PART ONE: EARLY LIFE

Failures and Football

Yes kids the "awkward" phase happens to all of us. In the case of my senior photo here, my "awkward" phase was that I was 17 and a beast on the football field, but unfortunately looked like I was 58yrs old and ready to sell you cheap insurance.

—Twitter, January 24, 2018

I fell in love with the game. It was more than that, actually. It gave my life a purpose. . . . Suddenly I had a chance to become the first person in my family to go to college. I became obsessed with making it.

—*Sports Illustrated*, December 5, 2016

Football was my ticket for my education . . . but I always knew, every time I stepped on the field, that I was always trying to catch up because I didn't have the football experience a lot of the guys had.

—*Sunday Sitdown*, May 2, 2021

I REMEMBER, AT that time thinking, well, all the heroes in my life are these guys. They're these guys who are big, they're strong. . . . I bet you if I built my body and if I went to the gym then I could change this scenario. So, from that moment, I think that defining moment now, years later, I fell in love with the game of football.

—*What Now? with Trevor Noah*, November 9, 2023

TO BE ABLE to go in a play with a swagger and confidence, and talk trash and be part of a winning program that was trailblazing at that time was important to me. That's the reason I signed up to play for Miami.

—*Sports Illustrated*, January 21, 2010

We would outwork every team in the country and every day we were committed to that mindset. In the weight room, outside of the weight room. In addition to we're gonna "hit, stick, and bust d--- and talk s---," which was a saying we had, in addition to that, we were gonna outwork everyone in this country. And my time at Miami helped me in terms of creating The Rock. Really talkin' trash in an over-the-top way.

—***Sports Illustrated,*** **January 21, 2010**

I wanted to play pro [football] and I also wanted to work for the Secret Service. And that's what I got my degree in, it was criminology.

—***The Ellen Show,*** **October 3, 2003**

In college, my goal was to eventually work for the CIA. Until my criminal justice professor and advisor (Dr. Paul Cromwell) convinced me that the best operative I could become for the agency is one that also had a law degree.

I thought that's a great idea until I realized no respectable law school would ever let me in with my pile of steaming shit grades.

—Instagram, June 12, 2018

For the record, I only received an A throughout my scholastic career just ONCE.

In college. Miami. Political Science.

Go figure.

—Twitter, July 30, 2022

Looking back - the most important parts of college for me were the times when I struggled. Hit rock bottom a time or two, was put on probation for breaking rules and was seconds away from losing my scholarship.

Life lessons I carry with me today.

—Instagram, September 17, 2023

My goal and my dream was to play pro football. . . . There are fifty-three men on an NFL roster; I was always number fifty-four. I was that guy that the coaches said, "DJ, you're good, but you're not good enough, and unfortunately, this is where the dream ends." . . . The chip that was put on my shoulder, and the fire and the drive, has led me here today.

—*Jimmy Kimmel Live*, July 21, 2022

We've all been cut from something, pushed to the side and told "fit in or you're not gonna make it."

I've built my careers on disruption, so I can tell you that the road is long and work is hard, but you can do it.

—Instagram, January 27, 2023

For me, wrestling never represented "that's massive success, that's where I need to go." It was always pro football. And I thought, if I can make it to the NFL, then I can buy my parents their first home, I can be the first one to go to college, I can have a little bit of money, more than seven bucks. And that never happened for me.

—*The Will Cain Show,* January 24, 2024

I ALWAYS SAY that making it to the NFL was the best thing that never happened to me. Cos it put a chip on my shoulder that never goes away. Helped shape me.

—Instagram, May 12, 2023

I GOT HURT, had injuries, I struggled, and I got depressed. . . . And when I eventually called it a day, I had to come home, move in with my parents. I was 24, living in a small apartment in Tampa with my folks.

—*British GQ,* November 15, 2016

WHEN I GOT cut from Canada [CFL], I had seven bucks in my pocket and I always tell that story, so now my production company is Seven Bucks, advertising agency is Seven Bucks, everything is Seven Bucks.

—The Rock YouTube channel, May 15, 2018

I ACTUALLY HAD $6 bucks and change, but at least I was financially optimistic and I rounded up to seven. $7 bucks.

—Twitter, March 22, 2022

BY 23YRS OLD, I failed at achieving the biggest dream of my life. My ass was kicked and I was down - but not out. I refused to give up, got back up and pushed on.

—Instagram, November 22, 2018

WHEN WE FAIL at something, not only does it define you, but you don't quite know . . . how important that failure is in that moment.

—*The Will Cain Show*, January 24, 2024

TAMPA FOR ALL of us became a very challenging place. My dad was not wrestling anymore, not making any money.

— The Rock YouTube channel, April 10, 2019

THE "EMBRACE YOUR failures" philosophy doesn't work for everybody, but it works for me and I'm sharing it with you. . . . Fell into my second bout with depression, but eventually my will was stronger than my emotional pain. I made a plan and put my two hands to work. My initial plan was to just pull myself up out of this sludge and shit and realize that I ain't throwing in the fucking towel.

Step by step, day by day, week by week, month by month, year by year... things got better.

My will found a way. Yours will too.

—Instagram, April 21, 2018

I MOVED BACK in with my parents, I felt like a failure, I became depressed—and it was at that point where I went through a little bit of probably a two- to three-month period where, you know, you're living in a sludge, man, you're feeling like shit, you're depressed, "what am I going to do"—and then I made a decision to start training for wrestling.

—***Jake's Takes*, April 15, 2011**

Part II

PART TWO: CAREER

Wrestling

Back when I was gettin' my ass kicked from life and had $7 bucks in my pocket, I would always think, "Man if I could just make it, I wouldn't have anymore stress and pressure." You work your ass off to "make it" but then I realized you gotta be even more hungrier and work even harder once you get there.

—Instagram, January 12, 2018

I was in the wrong game. And now I'm in the right one.

—*Sports Illustrated*, December 5, 2016

Growing up in a family of wrestling was, of course, incredibly influential to me because I fell in love with the business.

—*The Epic Journey of Dwayne "The Rock" Johnson*, 2012

My love for the WWE is endless. I grew up in the WWE. I was born into the WWE. My blood is the WWE.

—*Raw*, March 1, 2011

Truth is, I became a pro wrestler for two reasons...

I LOVED and have a PASSION for pro wrestling.

And I was tired of being fucking broke.

—Instagram, March 14, 2022

I've always been a performer. When I was eight years old, I used to crack up my family by doing Richard Pryor monologues. So the showmanship of wrestling came easy to me. I loved playing the heel because of the intense reaction it generated. That was my No. 1 thing every night: I just wanted to connect with the audience.

—*Sports Illustrated*, December 5, 2016

THAT GUY BACK then, oh, man. He was nervous as a motherfucker and didn't know what was going on. And he was flying by the seat of his pants.

—***Vanity Fair*, October 12, 2021**

BEFORE I HAD a shot at the WWE, I had to prove myself. . . . When you are continually scratching and scratching, trying to get ahead and make a living, you have to constantly think: how can I appeal to the audience?

—***British GQ*, November 15, 2016**

I THINK WRESTLING for $40 a night and eating at the Waffle House three times a day, wrestling every weekend at a flea market, then at a state fair or a car dealership or in barns, "blade jobs," where I cut my forehead with razor blades. . . . These days I never question, "Oh, do I deserve it?"

—***Esquire*, June 29, 2015**

I felt, in my gut, that I had something to offer in the world of pro wrestling. I didn't know what it was, I had no idea.

—*Sunday Sitdown,* May 2, 2021

WRESTLING ISN'T REAL, it is scripted; people know all this, so to make them care about you and your character, you have to connect with them somehow.

—***British GQ,*** **November 15, 2016**

AFTER I HAD my first wrestling match, in boots and purple shorts that I borrowed, I knew I was in love. I knew that with complete clarity. I didn't know if I would ever make it, but I did know I loved it.

—***British GQ,*** **November 15, 2016**

MY FIRST PAYCHECK was forty bucks.

—***The Pivot,*** **May 9, 2023**

There was a little voice that we always got to listen to and if we're lucky enough, if we're smart enough to listen to it, it could usually lead you down the right path of something good, so my gut was saying, "Business is calling. Wrestling is calling."

—*The Pivot*, May 9, 2023

Generally, when somebody comes in the WWE and they have their very first match, [it's] at a live event or at a very small venue. It's certainly not at a big pay-per-view. My very first match in the WWE was at one of their biggest pay-per-views of the year called Survivor Series in the most famous arena in the world, Madison Square Garden, where my grandfather wrestled in the '70s for Vince McMahon's dad, my dad wrestled for Vince McMahon in the '80s, and here I came in 1996.

—The Rock YouTube channel, October 4, 2016

I WAS GREEN as the grass and up until that point I had only wrestled in flea markets, state fairs and used car dealerships making $40 bucks per match. . . . On this night, in New York City, this punk kid with $7 bucks to his name and the world's worst ring wardrobe ever — got very lucky as 23,000+ passionate New York City fans embraced me like a son and the rest was blood, sweat & respect history.

—Instagram, November 18, 2018

THERE'S AN OLD saying in show business, if you can make it in New York, then you can make it anywhere. And my very first night in New York, they embraced me like a son and since then I have nothing but gratitude and love for New York City, for the WWE.

—The Rock YouTube channel, October 4, 2016

I WAS PLAYING this saccharine, plastic, big-smiling good guy and I was getting f-ing hammered every night. . . . I started getting pushed down the bill to take part in opening matches and then you begin to realize that your career is on the slide. They are not booing me as badly, because now they just don't give a f. And when that happens, you're done!

—*British GQ*, November 15, 2016

I GRAB THE microphone—the fans were already booing. They started chanting "Rocky sucks." I said, "I may be a lot of things, but sucks isn't one of them." In that moment, the Rock was born. And about a month later, I was the hottest heel in the company, and things were on fire.

—*Oprah's Master Class*, July 17, 2018

Even in the wild, unpredictable world of professional wrestling, there was a great benefit in playing a heel. I became, at that time, the best and greatest heel the company had going. That Attitude Era, I call it a very special time in the world of pro wrestling. The company wasn't publicly traded, so we flew under the radar. And some of the things—many of the things—that we were able to get away with, we'd be in big trouble these days. But that time as a heel really did teach me that you could do anything—as long as your reason why is relatable.

—*New York Times*, October 17, 2022

The Rock is a wild S.O.B. and at times, a complete lunatic who's given me everything-including the greatest gift of all...

Becoming The Rock allowed me to be myself

Authentic, real, grateful and crazy

—Instagram, January 31, 2024

THAT WAS THE most freeing thing for me and my career.

—on rebranding from "Rocky" to "the Rock,"
***The Joe Rogan Experience*, November 15, 2023**

THE ROCK WAS—still is in fact—the best role I will ever get to play. I was being me, but me turned all the way up to ten.

—*British GQ*, November 15, 2016

DOES THE ROCK slap hands and kiss babies and hug women? Hell no. Of course he doesn't do that. Does the Rock go out there and wink at the fans and entertain the fans? Absolutely. You're damn right. Because the Rock realizes exactly what we have here. . . . I'm saying, hey listen, this is sports entertainment. And the Rock is king at sports entertainment.

—*WWF: The Rock - Know Your Role*, 1999

When it's all said and done, and all the smoke has cleared, all the Rock's sweat, blood, and tears have fallen, they're going to realize exactly why the Rock is the great one, the chosen one, the people's choice, and the people's champ. Because the Rock will live, breathe, and die to do exactly one thing. And that's to entertain the millions and the millions of the Rock's fans, if you smell what the Rock is cooking.

—*WWF: The Rock - Know Your Role*, 1999

Fifty years from now, when the Rock is eighty years old, when the Rock has to put in the people's dentures, he's got to use the people's walker to come walking down that ramp, just like that, the Rock will still step right in the middle of this ring and say: Just bring it.

—*Raw*, June 17, 2002

Before the Nation, it was really no surprise, there wasn't a lot of depth to the character of the Rock. When the Rock joined the Nation is essentially when the Rock blossomed, when the Rock started.

—on the pro wrestling faction The Nation of Domination, *WWF: The Rock - Know Your Role*, 1999

The Rock truly means this. Dwayne Johnson truly means this. Whether I'm a baby face or whether I'm a heel, whether they accept me or whether they don't, the Rock will always go out there and he'll do his thing. You want to chant "Rocky sucks," that's fine. You want to chant "Rocky," well that's fine too. Doesn't really matter. But the Rock has the ability to make you chant something, and night in and night out, you'll see what that is.

—*WWF: The Rock - Know Your Role*, 1999

It never mattered to the Rock what number he came in. Whether it was number thirteen, number three, or three thousand. The only thing that mattered to the Rock is that the Rock went in there and was kicking that ass.

—*Raw*, January 22, 2001

I loved wrestling. I love the antics of it. I love the characters of it.

—*What Now? with Trevor Noah*, November 9, 2023

Being the WWF champion solidifies the fact that you are at the mountaintop, solidifies the fact that you grabbed that brass ring. It's something I worked very hard for my entire life, because I grew up in the industry.

—*WWF SmackDown*, March 22, 2001

I LEFT WHEN I was on top, like number one in the wrestling business, and I left. It was a ballsy, gutsy, some call it stupid move, but I had to commit and I had to follow what was in my gut.

—The Rock YouTube channel, May 29, 2018

MY WRESTLING CAREER ended the only way I was willing — flat on my back, getting beat 1, 2, 3, looking up at the stars and being grateful for my blessings.

I went out the right way.

The respectful way.

—Instagram, May 17, 2020

Here's the thing. You can design something to go a certain way, but at the end of the day—whether it's the Golden Era of wrestling . . . whether it's the Attitude Era, whether it's the PG Era—you want to look back in our business of professional wrestling. If you're not authentic, then you're done.

—*The Epic Journey of Dwayne "The Rock" Johnson*, 2012

WWE universe is a family, my family, has always been my family. I never left. I was quiet for some time, but I was doing something that I loved. I never ever wanted to utilize and leverage the WWE, or the fans, to help my movie career.

—*The Epic Journey of Dwayne "The Rock" Johnson*, 2012

For those of you who don't know, the Rock has many nicknames. The Great One. The Most Electrifying Man in All of Entertainment. The People's Champion. But I want to tell you something that's important to me right now. I need to take this moment, and I need to tell you something as Dwayne. It's been a long time since I've been back. Seven years, to be exact. But I want to take this moment, in the middle of this ring, to tell you why I'm back. . . . I am back in this ring because of you. When I left the WWE seven years ago, I dreamed big. And you guys dreamed big with me. You helped me accomplish my goals, accomplish my dreams, because you never left my side. And I want to take this moment to tell you all here, live here, millions watching around the world. I want to tell you thank you, I love you, and it is because of you that I am back in this ring, and it is because of you—and I give you my word—I am never, ever going away.

—*Raw*, February 14, 2011

THERE IS NO accolade on this earth that is more deeply engrained in my blood than this WWE Championship. From 1998 to 2003 I had the honor of winning seven WWE Championships. And after ten long years, I can honestly tell you that this moment, here with you tonight, is the proudest moment of my career.

—after winning the WWE championship and stripping "CM Punk" Phillip Jack Brooks of the title he'd held for 434 days, *WWE Live*, January 28, 2013

AT THE END of the day, the best part about me going back was the reaction and the response with the fans. That's it. It's not for money, not for any other reason—just for that.

—entertainment.ie YouTube channel, April 21, 2011

LORDY THE SH*T I'd say back then. Keep in mind I never cared about being the angriest or toughest. Just wanted to be the most entertaining.

—Twitter, November 17, 2016

My goal was just to entertain the fans. I didn't want to be the loudest, I didn't want to be the biggest. But I did want to be the best, and I did want to be the most entertaining. And I wanted to go into every performance without inhibition. And I always thought, every single night, there is nothing that I won't try. I will try it. I gonna try it and see how it sticks.

—*The Epic Journey of Dwayne "The Rock" Johnson*, 2012

I was born in this business. And they [the audience] know my heart and my soul is in this business. And they also know that I am standing in the middle of this ring, right now, in front of the world live, for no other reason other than I love the WWE. And I will always be a part of the WWE, and the WWE will always be a part of me.

—*Raw*, February 28, 2012

PART TWO: CAREER

Hollywood

THE INTENTION IN 1999 was to entertain. My intention in 2005 was to entertain. My intention in 2010, as the Tooth Fairy, is to entertain and make you laugh.

—*Sports Illustrated*, January 21, 2010

AS A KID, every Sat I'd go to the movies. Dreamt of being Indiana Jones or Rocky Balboa. Now here I am on set.

—Twitter, October 6, 2012

IN THE RING, we're able to tell a story every single night. In movies, it's nothing greater than telling these elongated stories in such great detail.

—*Ebony Magazine*, July 2001

I'VE BEEN FORTUNATE to have had the life I had prior to Hollywood. I wasn't starving, I was going to eat the next day. I came to Hollywood wanting a career that had longevity, and I wasn't afraid to take risks because I had a dollar in the bank. I wasn't driven by money as much as I was driven by making a successful transition. And I was smart enough to know that I certainly didn't have all the answers and I need to surround myself with smart people and be willing to take risks and be willing to fail.

—*Esquire*, June 29, 2015

LORNE MICHAELS AND *Saturday Night Live* gave me a shot, and at that time no one really knew who I was, I was popular in wrestling and maybe I was just a popular guy at that time, but who knows, maybe I would have fizzled out or not had a career, but those guys took a chance and those guys gave me an opportunity to host. When I hosted my first show at *Saturday Night Live* almost fifteen years ago, it opened so many doors.

—The Rock YouTube channel, May 19, 2017

I THOUGHT I could be good, I had a gut feeling, but I didn't know if I had what it takes. And I asked Ron [Meyer, president of Universal Studios] what I should do, and he said, "Look, you need to learn the business . . . but you have something. You have the potential to be special."

—*British GQ*, November 15, 2016

I SHAKE MY head in disbelief when I think about [the] journey it took to get here. When I first broke into Hollywood, there was no blueprint for me to follow for the half Samoan, half Black pro wrestler with a little bit of talent and a nutty work ethic.

Grit and gratitude.

—Instagram, March 12, 2023

"Let me just follow the half-black and half-Samoan actor who was also a wrestler. Let me follow his path." That wasn't an option, that wasn't there. So I was forced to create my own. . . . I don't just want to play the game. I want to change the way the game is played.

—Associated Press, April 26, 2017

I was looked down upon when I came into Hollywood.

—*Sunday Sitdown*, May 2, 2021

When I first got to Hollywood - all the "experts" told me, I shouldn't call myself The Rock, I shouldn't go to the gym and needed to lose weight - and definitely don't talk about pro wrestling. . . . That never sat right with me, so I said I'm not doing that.

—Instagram, October 2, 2022

I WAS AND still am, a walking contradiction who was willing to open my mind like a sponge to learn, put in the hard work, take the big risks and eventually I figured out that the most powerful thing I could ever be to Hollywood and the world - is myself.

—Instagram, June 14, 2019

YEARS AGO WHEN I set out to establish myself globally, I knew the odds were stacked against me, because I wasn't going into all these territories around the world as a superhero for Marvel or DC or an established IP backing me like a Harry Potter, Hunger Games etc. I was going around the world as just me, Dwayne Johnson - the big, brown, bald, tattooed human being. Who laughs a lot, drinks a lil' too much and cusses even more.

—Instagram, April 16, 2018

When I first made the transition, it was met with reticence and resistance. And I understood that—and I just felt like I had to plow through it.

—HeyUGuys YouTube channel, March 20, 2013

I can look back on that and make fun of some of the scenes in the movie but I will say this: I so appreciate everybody's support back then, because that movie led to another movie which led to another movie.

—on *The Scorpion King*, The Rock YouTube channel, April 4, 2017

I KNEW NOTHING about acting or the business of Hollywood. Nothing. The only thing I knew and was 100% committed to was surrounding myself with good hard working people and the hard work I was willing to put in with my own two hands.

I wanted to win, but I was willing to fail, because I knew that my effort was the only thing I could always control. And if I got my ass kicked and failed but gave great effort, I'd always come out the other side a better man.

—Instagram, December 17, 2017

I THOUGHT, "WELL, if I suck at this thing, and suck at the movie business, at least I'm gonna go down knowing that I gave one hundred percent effort and I put in the work with my two hands, and that's really the only thing I could've done."

—kinowetter YouTube channel, April 13, 2017

I TRUSTED MY instinct and I realized, just like in wrestling, I had to be me. The only problem was it took me five years to act on it.

—***British GQ*, November 15, 2016**

I DON'T LIKE to feel like I have constraints on or am trying to fit a mold or "This is how it's done, so this is how you should do it." I do have a little bit of a challenge with that. Maybe a lot of a challenge. And so when they say, "Dial it back," I say, "Sure! Watch this!"

—***Vanity Fair*, October 12, 2021**

IT'S MY GOAL as an actor to grow and just get better and try different things.

—Universal Pictures UK Youtube channel, May 10, 2011

WITH *THE Mummy Returns*, my expectations were, I just wanted to put in a good performance. I had waited for such a long time to break into Hollywood. I wanted movies. I wanted the big screen. That was my goal. I wanted that. When I was eight years old, I saw Harrison Ford in *Indiana Jones*. I wanted that.

—*The Epic Journey of Dwayne "The Rock" Johnson*, 2012

I'VE ALWAYS BEEN inspired by Hercules. . . . It was the first project that I brought up when I got to Hollywood fourteen, fifteen years ago. . . . I went to Brett Ratner's house, we had a great meeting, and I said: I was born to play this role.

—*BlackTree TV*, July 21, 2014

AS AN ACTOR, not showing my chiseled, extraordinary, handsome face was a tremendous sacrifice for me.

—on growing out his hair to play Hercules, Associated Press, March 25, 2014

The most important thing about the movies that we make—especially with the Fast and Furious franchise—is that the movie's fun. It's gotta be fun.

—*The Fate of the Furious* world premiere, April 11, 2017

I'm committed, of course—yeah, I would give [my physique] up for a role if it was something that I was passionate about, and, more importantly than my passion, to be honest with you, if it's something that I felt the audience really wanted to see.

—*Jake's Takes*, July 27, 2019

When you care about the characters, then you have a shot at creating a movie that stands the test of time.

—Dan Brightmore YouTube channel, May 28, 2015

I ALWAYS THINK that the best and greatest bad guys, bad girls and villains out there are coming from a place of truth. So one of the cool things that being a great bad guy and a great villain offers . . . [is] you get the opportunity to say and do a lot of things that people can't. A lot of people wish they can, but they don't.

—Associated Press, February 18, 2024

THE GREATEST OF villains have the greatest capacity and quality and depth.

—Arvind KAMALA YouTube channel, July 16, 2017

BEING THE VILLAIN is the greatest thing in the world. Everybody wants to be a good guy or good girl, everyone wants to be loved and cheered and considered the hero, which is great and it's natural; it's just human psychology and desire.

—Associated Press, February 18, 2024

It's really in our interpretation and who we deem a hero. Yes, of course, Black Adam in the mythology is a villain; or he can be considered an antihero, or to some he's a hero, to some who have a black heart like me!

—The Rock YouTube channel, February 17, 2017

The truth is, you know, we have stunt doubles and we have wonderful visual effects, because these movies are big-budget, but—I insisted I do that myself, so I literally slid on the ice and redirected a torpedo—with one hand!

—*TODAY*, April 7, 2017

It's whatever the biggest weapon is, point it in my direction . . . the basic tenet of screenwriting for a Dwayne Johnson movie, apparently.

—BBC Radio 1, November 12, 2021

THE BIG SPECIAL effects, and the spectacle . . . that's going to bring the audiences in. If we develop characters that people care about—that's going to hold the audiences in.

—*TODAY,* May 20, 2015

I DIDN'T WANT to only make action movies. I wanted to grow as an actor, and I wanted to work in all different genres. . . . The most important thing to me is to have diversity in terms of the filmography. That's important to me.

—*Jake's Takes,* January 11, 2010

WHEN A FAMILY movie is done right, everybody in the family has some character they can relate to on screen. . . . That's what family is all about—struggle, perseverance, staying together.

—*Orange County Register,* March 9, 2009

When you make a comedy, and especially if you have the interest in making people laugh and feel good, then that's what you do. You can't worry about looking cool. Rule number one, to me, in my approach to comedy: Don't worry about looking cool.

—*Entertainment Tonight*, January 14, 2010

There are a lot of actors . . . that utilize the platform of acting to explore their emotional shit. What has worked for me is a lighter touch. . . . I would prefer not to explore my emotional shit in my movies because for me, that's my responsibility to go figure out. . . . It's more important to me to impact as many people as possible on day one. I don't need acting to work out my personal shit. I work it out on my own."

—*Vanity Fair*, October 12, 2021

FILM . . . GIVES ME the biggest opportunity to make the biggest impact—global impact. I don't want to make small movies. I love and respect our movie business, but I want to make big movies. . . . It's the idea that I can impact as many people as possible with a big global movie. . . . I know I'm impacting people around the world by giving them some good entertainment.

—The Rock YouTube channel, May 20, 2018

YOU'RE ALWAYS GOING to have haters, and haters are like, "Well goddamn, man, how many movies are you going to make, how much shit are you going to do, you do a lot of shit!" I say, "Yes, that's my ambition, of course, why not? I can do it. Yeah, I love what I do!"

—The Rock YouTube channel, May 29, 2018

We do feel at Seven Bucks that we could do anything and everything as long as it's good, as long as it's quality—because really, that's the thing that we really sink our teeth into with the consumers and the audience and the people, is we're going to deliver quality to you, regardless of what genre it is, regardless of what area it is in.

—*SWAY'S UNIVERSE*, October 15, 2022

You hope you make something good, you surround yourself with the best people in the business—the best crew, storytellers—and you cross your fingers, you put in the work.

—Rotten Tomatoes, July 29, 2021

Box office revenues are cool, but the thing that really matters is the blessing to positively influence and impact generations along the way.

—Twitter, June 13, 2019

Most important relationship I have in this business, will always be the one I have with my audience.

—Instagram, May 20, 2018

The challenge is doing my best to stay 50,000 feet up in the air and have a nice vision of what the landscape looks like for the next year to three years. It's hard to anticipate trends and what the audience is going to like, but you always want to stay above the fray and above the weeds.

—*Variety*, December 13, 2017

For years I've built a trust with [the audience] that they're gonna come to my movies and feel good. So every once in a while, you have to drop this card, which is: You're gonna have to find another actor. We need to figure something out, otherwise I'm not gonna do the movie.

—*Rolling Stone*, April 4, 2018

I DON'T LIKE a sad ending. Life brings that shit—I don't want it in my movies. When the credits roll, I want to feel great.

—*Rolling Stone*, April 4, 2018

I LOVE BEING able to create big movies or TV shows that entertain people, that make them happy. . . . If you're going to pay for your ticket, that inspires me to want to make a great movie.

—Associated Press, April 26, 2017

FROM A TEENAGER who was arrested multiple times for fighting, theft and other fun stuff — to now being known as "the nicest man in Hollywood."

I'd say that kid did alright.

—Facebook, April 3, 2023

My work, my goal, my life, it's like a treadmill. And there's no 'stop' button on my treadmill. Once I get on, I just keep going and going. I want to do more in the WWF. I want to do more in the movie industry. Ultimately, I want to be the most electrifying man in sports entertainment, period.

—***Ebony Magazine*, July 2001**

PART TWO: CAREER

Business

I CONSIDER MYSELF an industrialist and an entrepreneur and a businessman as well. And I'm in the relationship business. I'm in the customer service business. I'm in the consumer product business. And I'm certainly in the movie business.

—*Vanity Fair*, October 12, 2021

I DEFINE SUCCESS by having a positive influence on people, and in the world of entertainment—that is a small sector, but yet it can be very influential—and my goal in terms of the things that I do on this side of entertainment, and some of the other businesses that I've started, is—the key, the number one anchoring element, is to always make sure that people walk away feeling good.

—*Insight with Chris Van Vliet*, October 11, 2022

Everything I do is considered - no action is ever by accident.

Sometimes you find success and sometimes you don't, but my satisfaction is knowing I'll always control my effort with my own two hands.

Forward thinking always wins the long term game my friends.

—Instagram, August 4, 2018

It's hard to stay ahead of the game. . . . You want to make sure that you're putting out content for people that they don't get tired of, that feels fresh, that feels cool. . . . It's constant.

***—BlackTree TV*, April 11, 2015**

I really try to make sure that I'm looking at the schedule and try to be smart about the moves these days. And I also learned there's just power in saying no.

***—The Joe Rogan Experience*, November 15, 2023**

REACHED A POINT in my career where my most important currency, is my time. . . . Be protective of your time. It's the one thing we can control where it goes and who gets it.

—Instagram, February 15, 2018

I THINK THESE days there could be a tendency for people to think that things come easy. It does not. No, it's actually quite the opposite. I stay up at night, putting in the work, but also really deeply contemplating the next move, and the multiple moves, and the impact and effect that this one thing will have. If you've ever been hungry, then you'll never be full.

—*Vanity Fair*, October 12, 2021

I LOVE BUILDING. And I love creating products and brands that have a certain quality to them to deliver to people. . . . I love it. I love what I do. Honestly, I love building from scratch with these two old dinosaur hands.

—*Vanity Fair*, October 12, 2021

I've always been very passionate about tequila . . . but this idea of creating a tequila brand was something that I had thought about almost ten years ago.

—***Sunday Sitdown*, May 2, 2021**

The biggest obstacle with [the Rock's tequila brand] Teremana was the wild convergence of us releasing Teremana into the marketplace right when COVID hit our shores. So we were impacted, of course the world was impacted, that's just one of those things where you really just had to sit back as a brand and go well, . . . the most important thing now is to take care of our families and try to keep them as healthy and as safe as possible, shut all of our businesses down.

—The Rock YouTube channel, March 16, 2021

We were trying to figure out a way to infuse *mana* and spirit and authenticity to the Earth out of Mexico, and out of respect to Mexico.

—***Sunday Sitdown*, May 2, 2021**

THIS WORD, TIJASI, is the first two letters of the three names of my daughters. . . . It gives the viewers and the consumers an idea that this is a legacy brand for me.

—on the word printed on the bottom of his tequila bottles, *Sunday Sitdown*, May 2, 2021

OUR [SEVEN BUCKS Productions] symbol is the Warrior's Face in battle. Emblematic of strength, protection, pride, love & MANA.

[It] also rests over my heart as part of my tattoo that symbolically tells a very detailed story of my life.

—Twitter, March 22, 2022

Maybe there's some takeaway value from my experiences that may help anyone watching. If you're lucky enough to become successful at something - go build more mountain and bring everyone with you.

Stand up for what you believe in.

Don't take no shit.

And always keep giving back.

—Instagram, December 2, 2023

I think when you're a good-quality human being in your DNA and your constitution, it leads to more effective decision-making.

—*Rolling Stone*, April 4, 2018

TRUTH IS, BEHIND my curtain are hundreds of people (maybe thousands if I stop and do the math) who share in this honor. I may be forward/consumer facing but success never happens alone.

Smart, hungry team.

—on being named one of *Variety*'s Top 500 Entertainment Business Leaders, Twitter, December 21, 2021

ANYTIME YOU LOOK to build anything out, it takes time. We play the long game. We've always played the long game.

—*GQ Sports*, May 15, 2023

THESE DAYS, I know what I don't know. And in a lot of these ventures I may not know a lot of things but I do know I need to surround myself with the right people, the brightest people, the hungriest people, and we go to work.

—*Sunday Sitdown*, May 2, 2021

I DIDN'T KNOW he would be a lifelong collaborator. He was 14 and I was 18, so we were just two punk kids talking shit to each other about who was better at video games. It was in the wild world of pro wrestling where Hiram cut his creative teeth and worked very closely with me. Even at that time we were always talking about the idea of growing.

—on his ex-brother-in-law and head of production at Seven Bucks Productions, *Variety*, July 30, 2019

I'M AN INDUSTRIALIST, entrepreneur & business man.

Customer service & consumer products business.

But most importantly, the relationship business.

To me, that's the backbone and MANA of all business ventures ~ the relationship.

—Twitter, October 19, 2021

We want to make sure that we have people around us who are inspired to do well and reach for and continue to share our vision, but also, at times, say "I'm not too sure if that's the right thing to do."

—***Oprah's Super Soul*, January 29, 2020**

I like to look and search for the good stuff that's out there, the stuff that's going to make me better, help me stretch out my aperture.

—***The Joe Rogan Experience*, November 15, 2023**

I started wrestling in flea markets before I got to the WWE. Even in front of 50 people, it was all about sending them home happy. And it's the exact same thing with the XFL.

—***GQ Sports*, May 15, 2023**

Do today what they won't, so tomorrow you accomplish what they can't.

—Twitter, December 3, 2012

[As] an XFL owner, I'm motivated to create as many opportunities for players as possible and advance & expand the game of football.

—Twitter, February 21, 2022

Whether it's acting, or wrestling, or producing, or any of the other businesses or investments, it just has to have connective tissue to me and the things I love.

***—Oprah's Super Soul,* January 29, 2020**

I like the idea that any project I touch, there is a general sense of action begets action. Hard work begets results. And there is some optimism. And a dirty joke.

***—New York Times,* May 20, 2015**

IT ALL COMES down to your family, and working hard to love and protect and do everything that you can to make your family, and the ones you love—their lives better.

—Hollywood Walk of Fame ceremony, December 13, 2017

Part III

PART THREE: RELATIONSHIPS

Family

I DID KEEP my promise and bought my parents their very first house in 2000 (we lived in apartments & trailer parks our whole lives). Then [in] 2004 they divorced and [it] all went to hell but at least they enjoyed it for a while 🤣

—Twitter, May 4, 2021

I HAVE BEEN very lucky, and a benefactor of being raised by very strong women and surrounded by strong women.

—*Access Hollywood*, November 8, 2021

MY GRANDMOTHER, MY mom. My first wife, . . . my wife today, . . . my three daughters continue to influence and teach me.

—Associated Press, March 15, 2022

FOR STARTERS MY "sweet" grandmother was brought on extortion charges from the FBI.

"Bang bang" were her final words.

She beat the wrap but the feds came back around and seized all assets. She was homeless two years later.

—Twitter, May 4, 2021

MY GRANDMOTHER WAS the first female wrestling promoter.

—The Rock YouTube channel, February 16, 2021

MY GRANDMOTHER, LIA Maivia didn't f*ck around. She promoted wrestling with an iron fist and getting violent with the wrestlers if they "got outta line" was common. Behind closed doors. She was ruthless with everyone, but I was always her baby.

—Twitter, March 2, 2021

Yes, my grandma (toughest woman I've ever known) told me this all the time. She always said you're gonna make it and you will take us with you.

She never called me DJ, Dwayne or Dewey. She only called me Tuifea'i.

She was special. I miss her.

—Twitter, January 9, 2023

I always say, if you're lucky enough to have a good mom, then you got a pretty good shot at being a decent human being.

I sure as hell got lucky.

—Instagram, October 26, 2018

MAAAAN MY MOM has been thru it all...divorce, cancer, hit head on by a drunk driver, and even a suicide attempt back when I was 15.

She survived it ALL and ironically, though not surprisingly – my mom is THE kindest, most caring and JOYFUL human being I have ever met.

And still brings her ukulele everywhere we go.

—Instagram, March 23, 2021

MY DAD AND my grandfather are the cornerstones of my career. . . . When I stepped into a WWE ring for the first time in 1996, my sole purpose at that time was to just make my family proud.

—WWE Hall of Fame Class of 2008 ceremony, March 29, 2008

He was everything. He was compassionate. He was loving. Fierce. Extraordinarily loyal. He was a warrior who loved this business, loved his family even more. My grandfather's integrity in this business was unparalleled. When my family reflect on him, we discuss the fact that he had such a great effect on people's lives.

—on his grandfather, the great "High Chief" Peter Maivia, WWE Hall of Fame Class of 2008 ceremony, March 29, 2008

I miss my grandfather dearly.

The Samoan High Chief Peter Maivia.

Beautiful soul and loved by everyone but don't fuck with him. After being insulted he pulled a wrestler's eye out.

—Twitter, November 8, 2022

My grandfather was known as one of the toughest men in this business, ever. But what set him apart: He was the kindest.

—WWE Hall of Fame Class of 2008 ceremony, March 29, 2008

At a time of tremendous racial disparity, he was able to cross all lines and become one of the most dynamic and formidable performers of his time. I remember night after night, watching him perform all over the country, being awed by his quickness, by his agility. He was an amazing performer.

—on his father, Rocky "Soulman" Johnson, WWE Hall of Fame Class of 2008 ceremony, March 29, 2008

My dad was a hero to me. And I thought, like all professional wrestlers, he was larger than life.

—WWE Hall of Fame Class of 2008 ceremony, March 29, 2008

I learned so much from my dad on work ethic, discipline. Respect is given when it's earned. Be proud of who you are, be proud of your skin color.

—*What Now? with Trevor Noah*, November 9, 2023

HE CAME UP the hard way, and trail-blazed for all of us men of color—in any sport and level of entertainment. But it was also very important to him to pave the way for all men, any color—it didn't matter.... My regret in this life is that I never had the chance to say goodbye to him, because he died suddenly. I regret not reconciling our complicated father/son shit before I lost him. Raised me with tough fatherly love and an even tougher hand. The more I live life, the more grateful I am for it.

—TikTok, March 1, 2024

TO MY GUYS out there, if your old man is still around - consider it a blessing. Even if you and your dad are working thru some complicated shit. I've been there and I understand. But do your best to reconcile and get that drama behind you and get right with your dad.

—Facebook, June 19, 2023

THE IRONY IS I fucking idolized my dad as a boy. . . . And obviously that idealization started to wane over the years. But the older I got, and the more experienced I got, the more I could appreciate his love for me in that limited capacity.

—*Vanity Fair*, October 12, 2021

[MY DAD] LOVED us with the capacity of which [he] could - given all the givens.

Raised me with an iron hand and a tough complicated love.

A love that now, as a father and man, I've learned to refine as I raise my own children.

—Instagram, February 7, 2020

Sometimes when people like my dad, "pave the road" and trail-blaze, they often pay an emotional & physical price.

My dad would always say—people can't feel your pain, they can only see it—so why show them?

—Instagram, August 24, 2020

We had some good times. We had some rough times. We had some fighting times. . . . And the good stuff is what will always be in the forefront of my mind, because I recognize that in our complicated testosterone-driven relationship, some of the best parts of me that I've been fortunate to share with the world I get from him. The resilience, the work ethic, the "No one's gonna give it to you, so you got to get your ass out there and work it, earn respect" type of credo, I get from him. And I will always carry that with me.

—*Vanity Fair*, October 12, 2021

The day he died, that night I went to bed and I felt so grateful and moved . . . because I realized, I have a new relationship with you. In death, I have a new relationship with you; in spirit, I have a new relationship with you. Clean slate, no regrets, no pain, no anger, no complications, just me and you.

—***Oprah's Super Soul*, January 29, 2020**

I felt that he was proud of me when I became successful in an industry that he had given his life to.

—***Oprah's Super Soul*, January 29, 2020**

PART THREE: RELATIONSHIPS

Romance

I'VE KNOWN DANY [Garcia] since I was eighteen, we met at University of Miami. She was an amazing athlete too at Miami. We have worked together since, and we also have a daughter, Simone, together. She became the first woman to own a majority share of a professional football league in the United States. That is history-making, it's just so amazing.

—*Jimmy Kimmel Live*, July 21, 2022

HER PARENTS WERE Cuban immigrants who were adamant about being American. English was always the first language in their home. They wanted their children to assimilate, adapt, and succeed. What they did not want was their daughter dating me, a person of color. I was half-Black, and that made me an unsuitable suitor.

—*Ebony Magazine*, July 2001

WHILE MARRIAGE WASN'T in our cards, we did realize that well, wait a second—we have been building something here that's pretty cool. Marriage may not be in our cards, but building business can be.

—***SWAY'S UNIVERSE*, October 15, 2022**

WHEN YOU CAN skillfully communicate your feelings and your intentions, and you come to the table with your partner as you guys are either going through a separation or divorce. . . . If you can get through the sludge—and it requires great communication—then on the other side of that is usually some greatness. And it's usually, you find a nice common place where you can work with your ex, your spouse, your ex-spouse, and again, get to a good place and stay focused on whatever the goals are.

—***SWAY'S UNIVERSE*, October 15, 2022**

THAT'S A GOOD way to put it.

Ride or die.

She always had my back and I always got hers. Our marriage didn't work out but that's life. Our friendship and blended families became more important.

—Twitter, March 22, 2022

ONE OF THE most important things as we were going through the divorce process was, "We're friends." . . . Our marriage not working out was the best thing in so many ways. It allowed her to meet the love of her life and me to meet the love of my life.

—Associated Press, March 15, 2022

My divorce did a number on me. I wasn't fearful of getting married again, there was just some hesitancy. But Lauren [Hashian] was incredibly patient: "I love you, you love me, we have this amazing life together—no presh."

—*WSJ Magazine*, December 3, 2019

Within 30 seconds, I thought, Wow, this girl's stunning. At the time, I was going through my breakup with Dany, and she was just coming off a big breakup too. Ironically, when you're not looking for something, the power of the universe kind of takes over.

—*WSJ Magazine*, December 3, 2019

I think I have had to be nothing but myself with Lauren. And she has had to be nothing but herself with me.

—*Vanity Fair*, October 12, 2021

So I had done a little bit of ripping myself open to her and sharing the truth and feeling like, if we have a shot at a life together and if you're going to love me, then the best version that I could give that is worthy of your love is one that's truthful.

—*Vanity Fair,* October 12, 2021

I've learned the power that we have to make other people happy and content in a relationship.

—*Oprah's Master Class,* July 17, 2018

There's a comfort. We may argue, but truly within 10 minutes we pull ourselves out of it and find some humor in the things that we just said. Mainly the things that I just said.

—*People,* June 16, 2021

For us, it came down to communication. . . . Just communication and being really clear in the intention and the goals and making sure that me and my ex, you and your ex, or anybody out there watching and listening, is making sure that those goals are aligned—and by the way, if they're not, that's okay. It's okay. We can say goodbye, and wish them the best of luck, and we'll see you down the road.

—*SWAY'S UNIVERSE*, October 15, 2022

Word to the wise, when you have kids, the most important phrase you will learn to say to your post pregnancy mama is, "yes, love that's an excellent choice and I'll take care of that right away."

—Twitter, April 27, 2018

I WAS A nervous and scared first time father (because I didn't want to screw shit up due to my own strained relationship with my old man) but eventually I learned that leading with love, empathy and a lil' humor would always be some of my best assets.

—Instagram, October 22, 2019

PART THREE: RELATIONSHIPS

Children

One of the greatest moments of my life. Holding my babies tight, while their mama sings our national anthem to 70,000 proud & strong. What a feeling. I'm a lucky man & papa bear.

—Twitter, December 6, 2022

The relationship that I have with my daughters is really the most important thing that I have in my life. When I had my daughters is when I realized what love meant—and not only what love meant, but also what unconditional love is, and a true, authentic, unselfish love.

—ABC News, July 12, 2018

The saving grace for me has really been my daughters, the three of them, and being a girl dad.

—*The Pivot*, May 9, 2023

Every man wants a son, but every man needs a daughter.

—Twitter, January 13, 2020

Big daddy is completely surrounded by beautiful estrogen and loving, powerful female mana.

All girls. One dude. And a boy dog.

I wouldn't have it any other way.

—Instagram, December 11, 2017

With my daughters, I want to be as full and as present with the love that I give them.

—*Oprah's Super Soul,* January 29, 2020

I know what it's like to have that separation and not be there for the birthdays, not be there for the pickups, the drop offs, and everything else. And I didn't want that.

—*What Now? with Trevor Noah,* November 9, 2023

I AM THEIR model of what a man will be. I'm the first man in their life . . . I want to be that example for them.

—*What Now? with Trevor Noah*, November 9, 2023

I WANT TO raise my girls with all the stuff that I didn't get from my dad when I was growing up.

But I will also pass on to my daughters, all the invaluable qualities my dad passed on to me — grit, work ethic, hunger, cultural pride and even if the love is limited — it's still love and it's still powerful.

This is what we do, as fathers and men.

—Instagram, November 11, 2023

BEING A FATHER to my little girls is the most important thing in my life. To raise 'em and always be there, during these critical years in their life.

I know what it's like to not be there all the time as a father, because of an unrelenting work schedule.

I won't let that happen ever again.

—Instagram, October 9, 2022

I WAS RAISED and surrounded by strong, loving women all my life, but after participating in baby Tia's delivery, it's hard to express the new level of love, respect and admiration I have for [Lauren] and all mamas and women out there.

—Instagram, April 23, 2018

I HAD ANOTHER baby girl, yes I love and admire women and no, I've never been too embarrassed to buy tampons. Bring it on!

—Twitter, April 26, 2018

WHEN I HELD her when she was born, I held her in these two hands, and I said to her, "I will always, always take care of you. For the rest of your life, you are safe."

—*Oprah's Master Class*, July 17, 2018

THE MOST IMPORTANT takeaway here (for me) is how powerful being kind to someone can be. Especially being kind to a kid.

—Twitter, March 25, 2021

She can be anything she wants.

She can sit at any table.

She can trailblaze a path, while humbly and gratefully recognizing those before her who paved the way.

She and her big sister, Simone and her baby sister, Tiana Gia will always have a strong voice and always make a positive impact.

—Instagram, August 26, 2018

A daddy of all girls and no boys . . . universe has a funny sense of humor balancing out my testosterone that way.

—Twitter, December 16, 2017

You can be wired, as a lot of fathers are, to fix things. Just having an expanded capacity to listen and be more tender and gentle really gave me that ability to solve whatever the issue is, but *with* them compared to *for* them.

—*People*, June 17, 2021

My superpower as a dad is the ability to not figure out why I keep falling for the "Daddy close your eyes" trick and I get peanut butter in the face, my face drawn on, kicked in the nuts.

—*People*, October 13, 2022

Years later, when I have the blessing to become a dad . . . I turn to my daughters and it's, "Oh, you want to paint my face? Hit the paint. How many colors do you want to put on?"

—*What Now? with Trevor Noah*, November 9, 2023

PART THREE: RELATIONSHIPS

Role Models and Rivalries

I'm always happy to shine light on those who impacted my life early in my pro wrestling career. Bret Hart treated me so good, took me under his wing and gave me great advice. Respect the business, save your money and never let those assholes bring you down. The rest is history.

—Twitter, July 30, 2021

Bret Hart was a mentor to me when he didn't have to be and in our wild and intense world of pro wrestling, there weren't many "mentorship programs" back then. He gave me guidance and I'll always be grateful.

—Twitter, December 18, 2021

I can pull in inspiration from everybody who I have around me.

—The Rock YouTube channel, February 17, 2017

[Vince McMahon] was one of my greatest business mentors and a father figure. Not always the relationship one would want with their boss but the convergence of our lives made it to be. We laugh when we get together because we always pick right back up where we left off.

—Twitter, March 2, 2021

My action stars growing up, biggest influences on me—Harrison Ford, Clint Eastwood, Bruce Willis, certainly him. Big action stars of the '80s—Stallone, Schwarzenegger of course, Steve McQueen, Paul Newman for sure.

—kinowetter YouTube channel, July 9, 2018

My grandfather, High Chief Peter Maivia & his tag team partner Pat Patterson. Pat was a brilliant trailblazer who also was the first openly gay pro wrestler in the 70s. He was also one of my greatest mentors.

—Twitter, February 3, 2023

["Stone Cold" Steve Austin] was a HUGE INFLUENCE on my career and [with] our legendary feud we went on to become the biggest box office draw pro wrestling has ever seen.

—Twitter, April 18, 2021

Respect, always brother.

You [Ric Flair], Dusty, my dad, Muraco, Hawk, Animal, Piper, all you guys were my heroes. This pic was taken in 1984 ~ in Vegas at the NWA annual convention.

I was [a] pimply faced 12 year old with an afro and you were (and will always be) "The Man."

—Twitter, December 2, 2021

ONE OF THE biggest rivalries of all time. The jabroni-beating, pie-eating, trailblazing, eyebrow-raising, kicking doors down, ain't gonna stop, ain't gonna knock, Triple H get his monkey-ass kicked by the people's champ, the Rock.

—on "Triple H" Paul Levesque, *WWE*, October 10, 2018

EVEN THOUGH WE had agreed that I was going to win the match and he [Hulk Hogan] was going to pass the torch to me—the wrestling world is funny, and I've learned because I grew up in the wrestling business that you don't count your chickens until they hatch, they come out of the egg, and it's happening. So I wasn't assuming that I was going to win, I was just waiting for Hogan to give me the green light.

—The Rock YouTube channel, March 28, 2020

THAT WAS ONE of the most incredible nights I have ever had in my career, because the audience was one hundred percent invested in our match.

—on his match with Hulk Hogan at WrestleMania 18,
***The Epic Journey of Dwayne "The Rock" Johnson*, 2012**

I DECIDED TO come back to the WWE because the timing was right. And in order for me to sink my teeth into something great, I need a challenge. John Cena had built a great name for himself, and he became the face of the company. And it kind of organically worked out, that I could come back, get involved with John Cena, and give the fans something amazing.

***—The Epic Journey of Dwayne "The Rock" Johnson*, 2012**

YOU UNDERSTAND SOMETHING about me, John [Cena], understand this. You strip away Wrestlemania. You strip away the glitz, the glamor, the lights. You strip away Hollywood, the movies, the fame. You strip away the catchphrases. You strip away trending worldwide. You strip it all away. . . . At the Rock's core, the Rock is six-foot-four, two-hundred-and-sixty pounds of man that will rip your throat out. At your core, you will always be a little boy who will go down in history always as the Rock's bitch.

***—Raw*, March 7, 2012**

You also start to realize that having friends is so vitally important as you just get a little older, because you lean on each other, you can open up.

—*The Pivot*, May 9, 2023

I MISS THAT kind of stuff because it's been a while . . . since I worked out with the boys. Back when I was wrestling, we'd all work out together because we were traveling together. . . . But I miss that camaraderie.

—*The Joe Rogan Experience*, November 15, 2023

I'M CONSTANTLY SURROUNDED by beautiful, amazingly strong points of view—including my two-year-old—and the women in my life and my family continue to be my best source of inspiration.

—*Variety*, December 13, 2017

I KNEW THAT if I made it in Hollywood, outside of the WWE, then that meant one important thing: that I just opened the door for the WWE, held open the door for the entire WWE locker room that's there tonight. I helped open the door, John Cena, for you. Paved the way for you. And what do you do? You publicly insult and knock the People's Champion.

—*Raw*, March 1, 2011

IT GOT REALLY uncomfortable for a lot of people. And it gets uncomfortable for the fans—that they sense something. But then when it gets uncomfortable for the wrestlers and to the executives and the company, then it's something special.

—on beef with John Cena, *Washington Post*, September 16, 2014

It's an honor. I don't say that lightly, we all feel that way.... We really wanted to make a movie that... is something that would make Robin [Williams] proud. Robin influenced us tremendously.

—on *Jumanji*, Associated Press, December 20, 2017

I'd memorize these Richard Pryor monologues.... I'd sneak the tapes off and commit these long, vulgarity-laced monologues to memory. You memorize Richard and you learn timing.

—*Orange County Register*, March 9, 2009

Both guys I love, both guys I respect, I admire. We're great friends still to this day.

—on "Triple H" Paul Levesque and "Stone Cold" Steve Austin, The Rock YouTube channel, March 14, 2017

You're only as good as your opponent makes you look . . . so always take care of your opponent.

—Instagram, November 17, 2021

In the spirit of what we do, in our business of sports entertainment, after the cameras are done, after the smoke is cleared, they're done chanting your names. The rightful thing is always to extend a hand, and thank the other man for doing what they did.

—The Rock YouTube channel, September 30, 2016

You win - you hug and shake hands.

You lose - you hug and shake hands.

This respect policy brings out the best in people.

—Twitter, January 5, 2019

The matches that I won, it was very real. I legitimately beat those individuals. . . . The matches that I lost, everything in that match was fake. There's no way that I could ever lose!

—The Rock YouTube channel, March 14, 2017

Yesterday was the eighteenth anniversary, the match between myself and the immortal Hulk Hogan. Whoever wins will go down as the greatest wrestler in the history of professional wrestling. And I was so excited to get into the ring with Hogan, of course, because he was one of my heroes growing up. From the very first moment, we locked up in that match . . . so he gives me a bump, boom, I land on my back . . . and I got up and I had this look on my face like you just embarrassed the shit out of me in front of the world, in front of 68,000 people. By the time the match ended, when I gave him that lock bottom, I nipped up, and I hear him say that "people's elbow," and I knew what that meant, that meant you're winning.

—TikTok, March 20, 2020

THE IDEA OF wrestling [Hulk] Hogan and creating this match of who the greatest of all time would be, icon versus icon, was very, very special.

—*The Epic Journey of Dwayne "The Rock" Johnson*, 2012

FAVORITE WWE MOMENT would probably be . . . the matches I had with "Stone Cold" Steve Austin. Yeah, they were really good, and we just had a real special chemistry, and any time we got in the ring it created this kind of magic, and we broke a lot of records and pay-per-view records.

—The Rock YouTube channel, May 20, 2018

ME AND ["STONE Cold" Steve Austin] just had that intangible "magic" in the ring. Trust and chemistry. Highest grossing feud in [WWE] history.

—Twitter, November 17, 2016

WE WERE FIGHTING. We were animals. We were pit bulls. We were lions. We were all those things, all those aggressive animals that wanted to be number one. It was important. At that time, the company was trendsetting, and groundbreaking, and we were ushering in this incredible era. So it was important to me that I was the one leading the pack. I didn't want to be second when I knew first was available. And Steve Austin sure as hell didn't want to be second.

—*The Epic Journey of Dwayne "The Rock" Johnson*, 2012

THE ROCK'LL TELL you how he feels about Chris Jericho. Sick of the People's Eyebrow? No problem. Sick of the People's Elbow? No problem. Sick of the people? Problem. The Rock'll tell you about Chris Jericho: Canadian moose hunting, long-haired, Twisted Sister–wannabe, punk-ass bitch. If Jericho sticks his nose in the Rock's business one more time, he's bought himself a fresh, fresh, fresh brahma bull ass-kicking.

—*WWF*, March 12, 2013

SEEING AS THE Rock didn't win [the Royal Rumble], it could have been ["Stone Cold" Steve] Austin, . . . it could have been Drew Carey, it could have been Jim Carrey, it could have been Harry Caray himself coming back from the dead to win the Royal Rumble, and it wouldn't have made a damn bit of difference to the Rock.

—*Raw*, January 22, 2001

ANDRE [THE GIANT] was a hero of mine.

And for some reason he took a liking to me too & always treated me like his own son. Maybe because we both had afros.

—Twitter, March 30, 2021

I HAVE TWO: one is "Nature Boy" Ric Flair, the other one is Hulk Hogan, and those guys sit on my Mount Rushmore. I'm on the back of Mount Rushmore. I'm not even on the front. To me, in my opinion, I'm on the back, raising my eyebrow.

—on the greatest pro wrestler of all time, The Rock YouTube channel, March 28, 2020

Part IV

PART FOUR: PHILOSOPHY

Culture and Representation

I'VE ALWAYS BEEN connected to my cultures, my family, and my ancestors. But as you go down the road of life, you start to get more connected with your spirituality in that kind of way where you start to realize what *mana* actually means, you know?

—***Men's Health*, November 26, 2022**

FOR ME, *MANA* becomes my daily anchor, and it's a reminder of my cultures. It's a reminder of who I am; and it's a reminder to work hard, to be humble, to show gratitude; and it's a reminder to always connect with people.

—***Men's Health*, November 26, 2022**

MANA IS ALL around us. No matter what color we are or where we come from.

Its real. And if you really pay attention to it and embrace it...

it becomes our shared superpower - all of us. It's a force that disrupts the world in the most positive and electric way.

—Instagram, December 1, 2023

I USE THE word MANA when I FEEL something.

It's a Polynesian word that represents an ENERGY and a POWER.

—Instagram, October 16, 2022

I IDENTIFY AS exactly what I am - both. Equally proud. Black/Samoan.

—Twitter, March 19, 2019

I'M BIRACIAL, RIGHT—I'M Black Samoan . . . and oftentimes, when you're younger, we struggle sometimes with identity. "Oh, I wish I was a little bit more like that," or "I wish I wasn't different." But . . . you are most powerful, and most important is when we just embrace who we are.

—*BlackTree TV*, July 21, 2014

THE BEST THING that I could do is control the controllables . . . and if someone then continues to choose to discriminate against me, well, that's on them.

—*People*, June 16, 2021

WHEN I SAW my first "Black Adam" comic when I was a little boy, I thought he looked cool . . . but also, he had brown skin. . . . And I thought, I want to be that guy. That guy's a superhero, and he's got brown skin like me.

—*Good Morning America*, October 17, 2022

In Polynesian culture we have a belief, that something isn't done when it's ready... it's done when it's right.

—Instagram, August 29, 2018

On a personal scale, you know, this movie is deeply personal to me, not only because it's a character that I had just—I loved playing and creating over the years, in *Hobbs*, but then also, this is the very first time that I could showcase one of my cultures—I'm half Black and half Samoan—showcase one of my cultures on a massive scale like this, in *Hobbs & Shaw*.

—on *Hobbs & Shaw* world premiere, July 14, 2019

This story is my culture.... I wear this culture proudly on my skin and in my soul.

—on *Moana*, Associated Press, April 3, 2023

[The] Siva Tau; it's a dance, it's a ritual... it's like the Samoan version of the Haka.

—The Rock YouTube channel, July 31, 2019

My tattoo tells a powerful story of love, family & warrior spirit thru Polynesian symbols. My ink is my mana - my strength.

—Twitter, June 27, 2013

This tattoo tells the story of my life and everything that's important to me . . . there wasn't one moment that I thought, "Oh, I've earned it." It's just . . . there's a term we have in Polynesian culture, it's called *mana*, and *mana*—it's power, it's your spirit, and sometimes *mana* takes over, and then you just know, "It's time. It's time, it's time to get the tattoo."

—*FOX 5*, November 12, 2016

Eye is the mana - the spirit and the power. It's everything. It's where I draw my strength from all things I love and protect.

As with my Polynesian tattoo on the left side of body, the symbolic mana lays over my heart.

We all have mana. Our strength. You just have to find it.

—Instagram, November 27, 2017

The whole idea of creating this fund, The People's Fund to Maui, was to help people and help survivors. These are my people.

—on raising money to support Maui after devastating wildfires, *What Now? with Trevor Noah*, November 9, 2023

I'm proud of them. I'm so proud of our people. . . .it's what you do in times like this. You fucking come together.

—*The Joe Rogan Experience*, November 15, 2023

I ALWAYS SAY, "it's nice to be important, but more important to be nice."

I was told back then (by a few influential folks) that playing a gay man would "ruin my career."

I said "hold my tequila and f*ck off."

Nicely of course.

—on the film *Be Cool*, Twitter, July 31, 2022

OUR INDUSTRY HAS a responsibility to tell inclusive stories, and I hope my character in *Skyscraper* is an example of that commitment. I certainly encourage the entire (entertainment) industry to take steps forward to audition and cast actors with disabilities to play characters with and without disabilities. Disability is an essential piece of diversity, and our characters and actors should definitely 100 percent reflect this.

—Associated Press, July 12, 2018

I THINK WHAT'S gonna touch upon all of us, regardless of where we're at in the world—where we're from, cultures, class, religion—is the voice . . . the little voice that you always gotta listen to—your gut, your intuition. You can do things, you can go beyond boundaries, and you have to trust that gut and instinct.

—*Moana* press conference, November 19, 2016

WHAT I TOOK away from watching *Moana,* and my hope what people in the world will take away from watching *Moana,* is not only a better understanding of our [Polynesian] culture . . . but also they will take away the most important thing we all have: family. And the power of family, and the importance of family . . . don't ever forget where you came from, and always give back to where you came from, and always acknowledge where you came from.

—ScreenSlam YouTube channel, November 16, 2016

BLAST FROM THE past.

So much fun bringing the legendary demigod, Maui to life. On a personal level this film meant so much to me and my family, to be able to illuminate one of my cultures as well as young female empowerment.

—Twitter, February 2, 2022

WHAT'S CRITICAL IS the investment in more superhero characters of color, and Black Adam is one of them. It was extremely important to me and one of the reasons why I was not letting go.

—*New York Times*, October 17, 2022

WITH *HOBBS & Shaw*, I wanted to make a movie that had big action and that was a lot of fun for the audience, but also make a movie that had some real heart to it, and real authentic culture, and this philosophy that wherever your journeys take you around the world, life has a funny way, one way or the other, of bringing you right back home.

—The Rock YouTube channel, August 12, 2019

AS A BAD guy in the WWE, I used to call myself the People's Champion. . . . I realize that what it means to be the People's Champion is so much bigger than me. Because what it means . . . is you treat people good, you treat people kind, you take care of people, you are inclusive of people, all people, all colors.

—accepting the People's Champion Award at the People's Choice Awards, December 8, 2021

PART FOUR: PHILOSOPHY

Politics

Lots of crazy and hard stuff happening out there around the world. Headlines are noisy and comment sections can be toxic — but this is the reminder that there is still so much good in this world.

Heart, soul, mana, smiles & JOY.

—Facebook, December 5, 2023

Could I make a difference? Could I surround myself with really brilliant people to help me make decisions? Do I care about this country? . . . The answers continued to come up yes.

—*People*, November 15, 2016

I might win a race or two. I would make an entertaining president. Hey, people, [vote for me and] I'll lay the smackdown on taxes!

—*Ebony Magazine*, July 2001

If I do ever become POTUS, I'd be the first (and 💯 the last) to rock a fanny pack, mom jeans, pineapple haircut and raise a marginally talented, yet weirdly sexy eyebrow 🤨

—Twitter, June 18, 2022

I have a goal and an interest and ambition to unite our country.

—*Sunday Sitdown*, May 2, 2021

A year ago it started coming up more and more. There was a real sense of earnestness, which made me go home and think, "Let me really rethink my answer and make sure I am giving an answer that is truthful and also respectful." I didn't want to be flippant—"We'll have three days off for a weekend! No taxes!"

—*GQ*, May 10, 2017

I DON'T KNOW the first thing about politics. . . . I care deeply about our country. I care about every fucking American who bleeds red, and that's all of them. And—there's no delusion here—I may have some decent leadership qualities, but that doesn't necessarily make me a great presidential candidate. That's where I am today.

—*Vanity Fair*, October 12, 2021

I'M NOT SURE I even have the patience or resignation to deal with the B.S. that comes with politics.

—*People*, June 16, 2021

ALWAYS HUMBLING AND I'm so grateful to see polls and be asked about running for President.

But I want to raise my daughters, be there as their father and never be absent.

These are the critical years.

—Twitter, October 9, 2022

NOT SURE OUR Founding Fathers ever envisioned a six-four, bald, tattooed, half-Black, half-Samoan, tequila drinking, pick up truck driving, fanny pack wearing guy joining their club - but if it ever happens it'd be my honor to serve the people.

—Twitter, April 9, 2021

I'LL ALWAYS STAND for open dialogue and action - it's the only way to ensure bad history doesn't repeat itself.

When it comes to protecting our children, all bets are off and the responsibility lies with us adults and lawmakers to listen and do.

—Instagram, March 24, 2018

I DO BELIEVE that Election Day should be a federal holiday, paid, and really incentivize our Americans to get out there—and especially the ones who are unable to get away from their job—to vote.

—The Rock YouTube channel, September 27, 2020

I THINK WHEN human beings are in jeopardy, and they ask for help, good-quality human beings, whether locally or at the highest level of office, they help.

—*Rolling Stone*, April 4, 2018

I BELIEVE IN our national security to the core, but I don't believe in a "ban" that bans immigrants. I believe in inclusion. Our country was built on that, and it continues to be made strong by that. And the decision felt like a snap judgment. I feel like the majority of, if not all, Americans feel that protection is of huge importance. But the ideology and the execution [of national-security initiatives] is where we really have to be careful of not making those snap decisions, because there's a tail effect.

—on the "Muslim ban" enacted by President Trump, *GQ*, May 10, 2017

I'D LIKE TO see a greater leadership. When there's a disagreement, and you have a large group of people that you're in disagreement with—for example, the media—I feel like it informs me that I could be better. We all have issues, and we all gotta work our shit out. And I feel like one of the qualities of a great leader is not shutting people out. I miss that part. Even if we disagree, we've got to figure it out. Because otherwise I feel, as an American, all I hear and all I can see in the example you're setting is "Now I'm shutting you out. And you can't come." [Disagreement] informs us. The responsibility as president—I [would] take responsibility for everyone. *Especially* when you disagree with me. If there's a large number of people disagreeing, there might be something I'm not seeing, so let me see it. Let me understand it.

—*GQ*, May 10, 2017

PART FOUR: PHILOSOPHY

Health

Around 2008, 2009, I was going through a lot of personal shit that was really fucking me up. . . . Struggling to figure out what kind of dad am I gonna be. Realizing I'd done a piss-poor job of cultivating relationships, and a lot of my friends had fallen by the wayside. I was just scared. Personally, everything was in a very bad and challenging place. And then professionally, I couldn't bet on myself. I wasn't used to that. I'd always felt like I could put in the work and fix the scenario with my own two hands.

—*Rolling Stone*, April 4, 2018

I'VE WORKED HARD over the years to gain the emotional tools to work thru any mental pain that may come to test me. But years ago I didn't know what mental health struggle was. As men, we didn't talk about it. We just kept our head down and worked thru it. Not healthy but it's all we knew.

If you're going thru your own version of mental wellness turning into mental hell-ness, the most important thing you can do is talk to somebody.

It can't be fixed if you keep that pain inside.

—Twitter, May 12, 2023

WE ALL GO thru the sludge/shit and depression never discriminates. Took me a long time to realize it but the key is to not be afraid to open up. Especially us dudes have a tendency to keep it in. You're not alone.

—Twitter, April 2, 2018

We've always got to do our best to pay attention when other people are in pain. We have to help them through it and remind them they are not alone.

—*Express*, April 1, 2018

As an only child and someone who always kept all my shit inside (which can be damaging emotionally), it took me many years of life experience to understand and embrace the importance of opening up. Talking open[ly] about our mental health isn't a weakness.

It's a superpower.

—Twitter, February 2, 2022

While I don't know what it's like to experience OCD, I have had my own mental health challenges. As you know, laughter always has a way of helping us up out of the sludge of shit.

—Twitter, January 25, 2022

I feel comfortable in who I am. But it took a lot of time to get there.

—*British GQ,* November 15, 2016

In my head, the men I looked up to as being successful—in Hollywood at that time, Sylvester Stallone, Harrison Ford, Clint Eastwood—all had built bodies.

—*British GQ*, November 15, 2016

I still wake up in the morning with some deep-seated fear that I have to keep working out so that I don't get evicted tomorrow.

—*British GQ*, November 15, 2016

During those times when I fell into and was challenged by depression, the gym became my best friend. . . . You're able to go to the gym to sweat out toxins and get a little bit more clarity when you walk out the door. It doesn't fix the problem, but it helps.

—*Men's Health*, November 26, 2022

TRAINING FOR ME, or some sort of physical activity, has always been an anchor for me. It becomes my daily achievement.

—*Oprah's Master Class*, July 17, 2018

MY GYM TIME is really the only time I have an opportunity to be away from the public and by myself. So I get a lot of work done in here. Not only training. It becomes my meditation. Nobody bothers me here.

—*GQ*, May 10, 2017

I REALLY FEEL that there are fundamental skills that you learn in the gym in terms of discipline, working through your fatigue, pushing past what you perceive as a limit. 'Cause there's greatness on the other side.

—*Men's Health*, November 26, 2022

My philosophy is to eat clean and make sure that my diet is commensurate with my goals, which stay consistent throughout the year. It's better to stay in shape than to get in shape.

—*Men's Health*, November 26, 2022

Achieving and maintaining a certain aesthetic for months while filming is such a crazy science that requires constant strategy and a surgical eye from a great coach.

—Instagram, November 14, 2018

Whatever time my call time is . . . you back your clock up four hours, and then that's when I get up and train twice, or get my cardio in, and breakfast, and then I'll go hit the weights.

—*Extra*, March 26, 2013

I'VE GOT THIS thing where any time I go to bed—if I go to bed—I have to wake up before the sun. . . . If I don't get up before the sun's up, then I feel like the whole day's wasted.

—*The Backstage Experience*, April 6, 2015

I'M PUTTING ON my workout stuff and I'm tying my shoes and I'm like, shit, I should just call it a night. No one's ever gonna know, everyone's asleep. Maybe I'll just pick it up tomorrow. But I usually tell myself: Number one, I say, well, I try and remember what it was like when I didn't have much at all, those "seven bucks" days. I try to remember that, and usually that gets my ass in gear.

—TikTok, August 26, 2021

I'M NOT AN extreme guy, but I do get very disciplined and focused. Now, you take that discipline and focus, and you apply it to a cheat day . . . again, it's a cheat day, not a cheat meal. . . . It includes at least a dozen pancakes . . . four pizzas, two dozen brownies . . . and dominate everything.

—*Entertainment Tonight*, March 26, 2013

NOPE, I'M THE opposite of a "not washing themselves" celeb.

Shower (cold) when I roll outta bed to get my day rollin'.

Shower (warm) after my workout before work.

Shower (hot) after I get home from work.

Face wash, body wash, exfoliate and I sing (off key) in the shower.

—Twitter, August 6, 2021

I WORK OUT, I hydrate, I drink tequila. It's that simple.

—*WSJ Magazine*, December 3, 2019

IN EVERY COUNTRY, around the world, if there's a hardcore gym where I can jack iron... I'll find it.

—Instagram, July 5, 2018

THERE AIN'T NO chilled lemon water, fancy spa towels, TV's or mirrors on the walls waiting for you when you walk into my gym.

Just the opportunity to eat dirt, pay your dues and see progress.

Let's get to work my friends. Rents due.

—Instagram, December 23, 2017

I'M UNAPOLOGETIC IN the gym when I start to sense too much bullshitting and not enough getting work done.

If you see me working in the gym, just pass me on by and don't try and talk to me. Have some gym etiquette or I will stop what I'm doing and eat you for lunch.

—Instagram, November 17, 2017

I NEED EVERYTHING kept real and authentic.

My real gym. My real workout. My real sweat. My real music. My real cuss words.

—Instagram, June 16, 2018

PART FOUR: PHILOSOPHY

Perspective

I WAS BORN into this crazy world and I love every second of it.

—Instagram, February 11, 2024

DREAMS AIN'T JUST for dreamers. Especially the ones that don't come true. . . . I dreamed of walkin' down this tunnel and playing in the NFL.

After what felt like a lifetime of commitment and hard work, I failed to make it and that dream never came true. . . . Just wasn't meant to be and more importantly, I just wasn't playing the right game.

Raising a grateful glass of tequila to dreams that don't come true.

—Instagram, September 2, 2018

HERE'S MY TRUTH ~ my dream was never what I am today.

I'm so grateful to be where I'm at, however my driving ambition was this:

"I can not be fucking broke."

That's the truth and that's the chip that remains on my shoulder. So today, I scratch, claw, kick, claw, bite and fight to never have just $7 bucks again.

That feeling never goes away.

—Twitter, May 10, 2023

Keeping the hard times of my past, in the forefront of my mind.

As noisy and as busy as life is, this mentality allows me to always to walk with a greater, quieter clarity.

More important than money and way more important than fame - I can go into any and every scenario in my business knowing two critical things:

No will ever outwork me and my two hands.

And I already know what it's like to get my ass kicked, be down and have nothing - so bring it on.

—Instagram, September 4, 2018

I often think what I would say to my younger self. That young scared kid struggling to stay on the right path but not afraid to put in the work.

We did alright, kid.

—Twitter, April 13, 2023

I ALWAYS LOVE the idea of being fearless and what that means. I'd say, that's what I want, and I'm gonna attack it, and I'm gonna go after it, and I'm gonna make it, I'm gonna make it happen. And if that doesn't happen, I'm gonna create another opportunity where I'm gonna move the world.

—*The Epic Journey of Dwayne "The Rock" Johnson*, 2012

THERE WAS A time in my life when I wasn't too confident about the why, and why it was happening.

—*Oprah's Super Soul*, January 29, 2020

Like a lot of ya out there, I know what it's like to have the weight of the world on your shoulders, getting pulled in a 1000 different directions with an endless amount of people (and businesses) relying on you to deliver for them so they can feed their own families.

I got you. I live it.

—Instagram, September 18, 2018

Over time and experience, I've realized that the greatest benefit to fame is impacting people's lives in a positive way.

And over time I also realized that the thing that's more important than being famous for something — is being great at something.

—Instagram, September 23, 2023

You'll never hear me complain about fame. Ever.

Because I've lived the alternative when I wasn't famous and no one gave a shit and I was broke. Fame is a blessing.

—Facebook, August 29, 2023

Fame is tricky and hard to control if your feet aren't firmly planted on the ground. Anchors and perspective is always important. Humility and kindness matters.

—Twitter, September 25, 2023

I felt like I've always been very coachable in whatever it is that I did, whether it's football, wrestling, track, whatever it is.

—*The Joe Rogan Experience*, November 15, 2023

I HAVE VERY thick skin - and you can always count on me to be direct with my words.

—Twitter, December 20, 2022

IF ANYBODY IS rude, or anybody is treating other people rudely or unkindly, I'll happily step in. And they don't want any bit of this.

—The Rock YouTube channel, October 28, 2016

I AM SO grateful, I wake up every day, my heart is so full of gratitude for the position that I'm in, for the opportunities that I have, for the opportunities that I'm able to create.

—Hollywood Walk of Fame ceremony, December 13, 2017

YOU DON'T GET anywhere by yourself. You need a lot of people around you to have your back, and have your front.

—accepting the Inspirational Icon Award at the Grio Awards, November 25, 2023

Realized over the years that success doesn't change a person... it only magnifies who've they've been their entire life.

—**Twitter, February 25, 2014**

I DEFINE SUCCESS by having a positive influence on people. . . . And I also would define success by raising some good babies if you're fortunate enough to have some kids.

—*Insight with Chris Van Vliet*, October 11, 2022

FOR ME, I like to operate as if everything is a marathon, and I like to take my time and do things right, compared to the sprinting philosophy and try to get it done quick.

—The Rock YouTube channel, March 16, 2021

IT'S TAKEN ME years to realize but these days I always try to not be too attached to an exact end result. As you said, it can often look differently than how we imagined.

—Twitter, February 14, 2022

HAVING THE GUTS to fail is far more powerful than having the desire to succeed.

—Instagram, January 4, 2023

I LOVE WHEN things get uncomfortable, it forces me to disrupt to hold everyone and everything (especially myself) accountable to step the fuck up and get the job done.

—Instagram, August 7, 2021

LAUGHS AND SMILES aside - in life, when you tell us we can't do something, it becomes personal.

It's always personal.

—Twitter, September 17, 2023

TWO HAND PHILOSOPHY.

If I can't earn it, then I don't want it.

My hands might be calloused up and scarred up with a knuckle or two missing (poor punching form) but they're mine and serve as my daily anchors for puttin' in the work to [get] the job done.

Earn it.

Own it.

Be grateful for it.

—Instagram, September 12, 2018

I NEVER WANT to just play in the game... I want to change the way the game is played.

—Instagram, September 26, 2018

NO ONE WILL outwork me. No one.

—The Rock YouTube channel, May 20, 2018

IT'S WHAT I do. It's what I love to do. I love to entertain. I live to entertain—in the middle of this ring, movie screen, doesn't matter. I live to entertain.

—*Raw*, February 28, 2012

I'VE COME A long way from rockin' fanny packs to a big, brown, bald, tattooed style iconoclast. But I have learned, that "style" is never trying too hard - just be you. Confidence. Vibe. Soul. And always exfoliate fellas.

—Instagram, July 21, 2022

I NEVER EXPECTED in my wildest of wild dreams that I would ever be in a position to be on the cover of *PEOPLE*.

—*People*, June 16, 2021

1995 I HAD $7 bucks in my pocket. Today I'm on the *FORBES* 100 LIST. Honored.

—Twitter, May 16, 2012

PART FOUR: PHILOSOPHY

Fun

I LIKE FINDING the fun in things. You know, life is crazy, life is very busy, and we all got crazy responsibilities, and I like to try and find some humor in everything.

—JinnyboyTV Hangouts YouTube channel, April 11, 2017

THERE'S ALWAYS ROOM for a cheesy joke.

—TikTok, February 22, 2023

SENSE OF HUMOR is EVERYTHING when it comes to being sexy. Takin' yourself too serious = big turn off. Humor lifts all the other qualities.

—Twitter, November 15, 2016

IN A VERY non-egotistical way, my favorite memes are all the ones of myself. . . . There's one meme in particular that I love, it says "Let me stop you right there, before you assume I give a shit." I love that, I love that, because that's the world I live in!

—The Rock YouTube channel, April 18, 2017

My mind can be a very dangerous (and fun) place . . . just don't ask me about math, because I suck at that — everything else I'm brilliant at though.

—Instagram, December 31, 2018

Yeah I met the Rock too.

Great guy, smells awesome, super intelligent, wonderful dirty joke teller, trusted handshake and can look constipated when drunk.

—Twitter, February 11, 2023

And as for my favorite rock... well, from the three scientific classes of rocks - sedimentary, metamorphic & igneous. I would have to go with the big, brown, bald, tattooed Rock.

That's my favorite species of Rock.

—Twitter, April 27, 2020

Love the grammar citations, which I have received many over the years.

—Twitter, June 11, 2022

Honored [to] have a word actually make the dictionary.

Making my all my teachers very proud 😉🥃

For the record, I may have made the word "Jabroni" (a noun, btw) famous and part of 🌎 culture, BUT the Iron Sheik made it famous in our wild wrestling locker rooms!😉

—Twitter, September 1, 2020

When you've been up all night, they say nothing good happens at 4am.

I disagree, I've done lots of amazing things at 4am. True, tequila was involved but still.

—Instagram, October 20, 2017

Excuse me while I go back to being—what's that phrase? Oh, a bad motherfucker.

—The Rock YouTube channel, December 16, 2016

If the Rock had to guess why you're so angry, it's probably because nobody likes you and you're not funny. As a matter of fact, if you were one of the Rock's movies you would probably be *Baywatch*.

—*WWE*, January 1, 2024

The Rock ain't afraid of nobody. He ain't afraid of nothin'. The Rock has been beat before. But the Rock has whooped more ass than he's been beat, that's for sure.

—*WWE*, April 14, 2003

Now it's Me vs Sushi and in this game, there are no losers - only winners.

—Instagram, October 23, 2018

Yes, my friend.

This Rock devours cookies.

All kinds of cookies😈🍪

I'll introduce you to #CheatMeals and it'll change your life.

Tell Cookie Monster to move it over, cuz I'm coming to Sesame Street to kick ass and eat cookies.

And I'm almost all outta cookies.

—Twitter, January 6, 2022

THE MUSIC INDUSTRY describes me as "a one of kind, stylistic crooner with honey coated gravel for a voice." But they forgot to add that I also sing in keys that literally don't exist and purposely off tempo... all while sipping tequila for hours.

So if I ever sing to you and it sounds like something your ears have never heard before, well treat it like jazz and just go with it.

—Instagram, December 2, 2017

BACK OF THE jet is called, "DJ's Think Tank" where I get my work done, let creativity flow and stare out the window thinking intellectualized and profound thoughts like, If you could only smell like one food for the rest of your life, what would you want to smell like?

Tequila infused pineapple.

—Instagram, June 10, 2018

If you Hollywood visitors ever see a big ol' pick up truck rolling up on your tour bus—don't be afraid, it's just the People's Champ lookin' for free tacos and having fun.

—TikTok, September 25, 2023

That big kid who was willing to be the hardest worker in the room would go on to only become famous for wearing a fanny pack.

Seriously tho, what a grateful journey.

—Twitter, November 17, 2022

PART FOUR: PHILOSOPHY

Advice

I THINK ONE of the defining, seminal moments in my life was when I really realized the power and the value of asking for help.

—*Men's Health*, November 26, 2022

REALIZING THAT ASKING for help is actually the most powerful thing you can do and it's not a weakness. Men especially fall into this trap of being really averse to vulnerability.

—*People*, June 16, 2021

WE'RE ALL IN the same game, just different levels. Dealing with the same hell, just different devils.

—Instagram, April 8, 2018

SELF LOVE IS the hardest thing yet most critical. I'm working on it too daily. Never ends :). Self empathy is so important. You have the best day ever too!

—Twitter, December 30, 2019

EVERY KID STILL deserves a second shot. I got mine. I'm lucky. Look where I'm at.

—*East Bay Times*, September 15, 2006

IF I COULD go back and tell my high school self something . . . it would be: Even at your lowest point, things are going to be okay.

—*FOX 5*, March 20, 2015

THERE'S A LOT of you out there fighting for your dreams, so keep fighting. Sometimes the things we think we want most in life, are the best things that never happen. Then you find yourself on different roads, fighting for different dreams and knocking on different doors — that eventually open.

—Instagram, November 18, 2023

Hey young DJ, you can spend your whole life waiting to do something 'one day' or start living every day like it's Day One. One day or day one, you decide.

—Twitter, April 12, 2023

This is where this lesson transcended for me the world of wrestling, because I take this with me everywhere I go, in business, regardless of what it is, in film, in tequila, in whatever it is that I do, is the value in relationships of listening to your gut and listening to your instinct.

—The Rock YouTube channel, March 28, 2020

In real life, I can put on a MasterClass about the countless times I've had use my fear of something as a valuable weapon to overcome and succeed at it.

Or I failed.

Fear keeps us sharp - depending on how we use it.

—Twitter, September 8, 2019

The noise, the pressure, anxiety, and the stress is always going to be there, but the key is not to listen to the noise. Don't let it control you.

—The Rock YouTube channel, January 20, 2018

We're gonna have times in our lives where we get fucked up and knocked down. It's a very defining moment when that time comes because you can either say, "I'm done"... or you can fight thru your pain - physical or emotional - get back up and finish the job.

—Instagram, May 20, 2018

If you're lucky enough to get a little bit of success, and then you want to do something else that's not your forte . . . you're met with a lot of cynicism. . . . But you gotta fight through that, and you gotta listen to the voice inside, and then you gotta bring it. Just bring it.

—WSVN, November 12, 2016

THINK ABOUT IT... Our potential only ends, where our belief stops.

That 15yr old kid who had already been arrested multiple times, to the man I am today, will always be very surreal to me. . . . Forever a grateful man.

Shatter people's expectations and never limit yourself, because you never know how far your dreams will take you.

—Instagram, May 10, 2018

MORNIN' - BEING A true bad ass has no weight or gender requirement - just a 100% commitment to greatness.

—Twitter, May 10, 2011

STRONG BELIEVER IN the "Work begets work" philosophy. Work hard to create your opportunities. Think long term.

—Twitter, January 24, 2016

Success will always be driven by focus & effort — and we always control both.

—Instagram, September 20, 2018

When U walk up to opportunity's door - don't knock on it. Kick that bitch in, smile and introduce yourself.

—Twitter, October 1, 2011

You learn that there is no substitute for hard work, how important that is, and how important it is to set a goal, how important it is to work towards that goal, how important it is to think team first.

—*The Epic Journey of Dwayne "The Rock" Johnson*, 2012

ONCE YOU KNOW what it's like to truly be hungry, you'll never be full.

But when you operate daily as if you're f*cking starving for success, that's when your entire universe will shift.

—Instagram, September 8, 2018

OUTWORK ALL COMPETITION, be grateful for the grind, don't run from your demons and if it ever becomes personal, then payback's a bitch.

—Instagram, October 7, 2018

AT SOME POINT, you gotta be fucking tired of not being number one. You have to be, and you gotta fucking play angry. And I play angry.

—The Rock YouTube channel, May 29, 2018

May my face always serve as a reminder to everyone who walks thru your doors — to always be hungry, be humble and always be the hardest worker in the room.

And tequila. Drink lots of fine tequila.

—Instagram, November 29, 2018

Blood, sweat, and respect. The first two you give, the last one you earn. Let's get out and earn it, daily.

—The Rock YouTube channel, March 7, 2017

To me, life is action & faith. God, the universe (whatever your belief) will always meet you half way when you take that 1st step of action.

—Twitter, June 2, 2013

Work your ass off, be kind and enjoy your roses.

—Instagram, December 4, 2017

We all go thru the same complex shit, just different degrees of volume and intensity on a daily basis.

Take care of and protect your machine and find your anchor.

Because at the end of the day, regardless of how many people, businesses, co-workers, friends, advisors, teammates or loved ones you may have in your life - no one knows your machine and what it needs better than you.

—Instagram, October 15, 2017

One of my favorite quotes that I heard when I was fifteen . . . : "It's nice to be important, but it's more important to be nice."

—accepting the People's Champion Award at the People's Choice Awards, December 8, 2021

And man I'll tell you from experience - that the thing that actually matters most in life, isn't what your bank account says, what you do for a living, who you vote for or what kind of car you drive...

the thing that matters most in life, is how you make people feel.

How you treat EVERYONE.

—Facebook, April 3, 2023

Milestones

1972

- Dwayne Douglas Johnson is born on May 2 in Hayward, California. His parents are "Ata" Fitisemanu Maivia, from the Samoan Anoa'i wrestling family (via adoption), and "Soulman" Rocky Johnson, an Afro-Canadian professional wrestler and one of the first Black champions in WWE history.

1978

- Johnson's parents marry. An only child, Johnson grows up in poverty and a dysfunctional familial situation marked by Rocky Johnson's frequent absences and tough love.

1982

- Johnson's maternal grandfather and key paternal role model, wrestler "High Chief" Peter Maivia, dies of cancer. His death has a significant impact on ten-year-old Johnson, who starts getting in trouble and starts down the road to becoming a "very angry teenager." The Johnsons move frequently to find work, and as the perpetual new kid in school he often gets bullied by his peers and is often involved in fights.

1986–1987

- During most of Johnson's teenage years, the family barely scrapes by, and a young Johnson soon turns to illegal activities as a means to earn money to buy the things he needs. While living in Hawaii at age fourteen, Johnson becomes part of an organized theft ring that targets tourists. His petty crime gets him in trouble with the law on multiple occasions.
- Johnson and his mother are evicted from their apartment in Hawaii. His mother is distraught, and the hopelessness of the situation is a defining moment for Johnson, who often refers to it as a particularly low point from which he derived motivation.
- Johnson is sent to Nashville, Tennessee, where his father is wrestling. His life of larceny continues (so do his arrests) and his parents' marriage grows increasingly rocky. There is a particularly distressing incident when Johnson's mother walks into the middle of a busy highway during a fight with her husband. Johnson is the one to retrieve her and help her to safety, and this experience deeply affects Johnson and complicates his relationship with Rocky.
- As a young teen, Johnson is already 6'4", weighs about 220 pounds, and grows a full mustache. His classmates think he's an undercover cop and distrust him.
- Johnson turns to the gym and begins building his body as a way to gain control over his chaotic life.

1988–1989

- The Johnsons move to Bethlehem, Pennsylvania. During his junior year at Freedom High School, coach Jody Cwik recruits him to the school's football team, an experience that Johnson credits with changing his life's trajectory. Coach Cwik becomes a strong male figure for Johnson who provides him with structure and discipline. Johnson stops getting in trouble and sees football as a way to improve his circumstances. By his senior year Johnson becomes one of the best defensive players in the country, receiving many scholarship offers from top football programs.

1990

- Johnson graduates from high school and accepts a full athletic scholarship from the University of Miami (UM). He becomes the first person in his family to attend college. He goes on to become one of UM's most prolific student speakers, often delivering positive messages about staying in school and avoiding drug use.

1991

- Johnson is part of the UM Hurricanes team that wins the 1991 NCAA national championship. But a serious shoulder injury sustained during his freshman year triggers his first episode of depression, which prompts him to move home and drop out of college. Compelled by his coach, Johnson comes back and manages to restore his grades and rejoin the team. Though his college football career never regains momentum, he still dreams of playing in the National Football League (NFL).

1995

- Johnson graduates with a bachelor's degree in general studies, dual majoring in criminology and physiology.
- Johnson goes undrafted in the NFL and signs with the Calgary Stampeders of the Canadian Football League (CFL) as a linebacker. He is soon relegated to the practice team, which pays little. Johnson shares a run-down apartment with three teammates, sleeping on a mattress he takes out of a dumpster, and surviving on ramen until he is cut a few months later.
- At age twenty-four and with seven dollars in his pocket, Johnson moves back with his parents, who now live in Tampa, Florida. Johnson describes it as one of the hardest, darkest periods of his life. Feeling like a failure, Johnson plunges into a deep depression. Johnson eventually overcomes it and decides to become a professional wrestler. Despite initial opposition, Johnson's father agrees to train him.

1996

- Johnson begins his career in wrestling's grueling lower leagues, performing at flea markets, state fairs, and used-car dealerships in small Southern towns under his real name. He briefly wrestles at the United States Wrestling Association (USWA) in Memphis under the ring name "Flex Kavana." He works primarily as part of a tag team with Bart

Sawyer, with whom he wins the USWA Tag Team Championship.

- Johnson makes his debut for the World Wrestling Federation (WWF) in Madison Square Garden, New York City. He is presented as "Rocky Maivia," a name that pays tribute to both his father and grandfather's ring names. During the event's finale, fans loudly side with the rookie Johnson as he defeats his opponents.

1997

- Johnson captures the WWF Intercontinental Championship within months of his debut in the WWF. He makes his WrestleMania debut the following month, and successfully defends his title.
- As the first third-generation wrestler in WWF history, he is aggressively pushed as a clean-cut "babyface" (a heroic character and crowd favorite) despite his wrestling inexperience, which generates a strong fan backlash that almost derails his incipient wrestling career. After a knee injury that takes Johnson out of the ring for a few months, the smiling, good-natured "Rocky Maivia" persona is sidelined in favor of a trash-talking "heel" (villain) character, and "The Rock" is born.
- Upon his heel turn, Johnson joins The Nation of Domination, an all-Black Nation of Islam-inspired group that antagonizes the fans. The jeering behavior leads to increased popularity, and Johnson soon becomes the hottest "bad guy" of WWF.

- Johnson and Dany Garcia get married on May 3, having first met when they were both student-athletes at the University of Miami.

1998

- Johnson captures the Intercontinental Championship for the second time. Eventually, Johnson overthrows the leader of The Nation of Domination, which starts to be referred to simply as "The Nation." Shortly after, Johnson is ousted from the stable, which effectively disbands. He feuds with the biggest stars of the WWF, bringing about high-profile rivalries with "Stone Cold" Steve Austin, Triple H, Chris Jericho, Mankind, and Ken Shamrock, among others, that define the Attitude Era of professional wrestling.
- Johnson defeats Mankind to win his first WWF Championship. He is the youngest champion in WWF history.

1999

- Johnson wins two more WWF Championships, as well as three WWF Tag Team Championships as part of the partnership "Rock 'n' Sock Connection" with wrestler Mankind.
- In his first foray in television, Johnson plays his father in an episode of *That '70s Show*. He also has a cameo on the crime thriller TV show *The Net*.

2000

- Johnson has a guest star role on a *Star Trek: Voyager* episode as an alien wrestler, earning him praise for his acting and wrestling moves.
- Johnson hosts *Saturday Night Live* for the first time. His appearance attracts around twenty million viewers and catches the eye of Hollywood producers.
- Johnson's co-written autobiography, *The Rock Says...*, is published. It's an entertaining, action-packed memoir that includes many of his famous wrestling catchphrases, and it becomes an instant *New York Times* bestseller.
- Keeping a childhood promise, Johnson buys his parents their very first house.
- Johnson wins his fourth and fifth WWF Championships, and, with The Undertaker, his fourth WWF Tag Team Championship.

2001

- Johnson captures his sixth championship but then loses his title to "Stone Cold" Steve Austin at WrestleMania 17, widely considered the greatest pay-per-view (PPV) event in WWF history.
- Johnson and Dany Garcia's daughter, Simone, is born on August 21.
- Johnson plays a small but memorable role as the Scorpion King in *The Mummy Returns*, his motion picture debut.

- With Chris Jericho, Johnson wins his last WWF Tag Team Championship.

2002

- Johnson plays his first leading role in *The Scorpion King,* which catapults him into Hollywood stardom. The movie earns more than $165 million worldwide, and his $5.5 million paycheck enters Guinness World Records for the highest salary paid to an actor in their debut starring role.
- Johnson and Hulk Hogan face each other at WrestleMania 18 in what's considered one of the most memorable matchups of all time. It's marketed as "Icon vs. Icon," and Johnson turns up victorious.
- Johnson earns his seventh WWE Championship. [The WWF rebrands this year as the World Wrestling Entertainment (WWE)].

2003

- Johnson stars in his next big feature, *The Rundown,* which earns positive reviews but is a box-office disappointment. Wrestling fans start to notice Johnson's shift from professional wrestler to Hollywood actor and begin to sour, booing him at every appearance. As a way to deal with the negative reactions, Johnson adopts the "Hollywood Rock" villainous persona. "Hollywood Rock" is arrogant and entitled, features a new shaved look and entrance song, and leans into everything the fans criticized about his emerging acting career—and they love it.

- On March 30, Johnson and "Stone Cold" Steve Austin face each other for the last time at WrestleMania 19, a match that ends their career-long feud.
- Johnson's parents, Rocky and Ata, get divorced.

2004

- Johnson retires from the WWE to focus on his acting career full-time.
- Johnson stars in the remake action film *Walking Tall.*

2005

- Johnson is cast in the crime comedy film *Be Cool* playing a gay Samoan bodyguard. Johnson's acting receives positive reviews, but the movie garners generally negative criticism. So does the videogame-to-film adaptation *Doom,* in which Johnson plays the main antagonist—in fact, it is later named one of the ten worst video game movies by *Time.*
- Attempting to conform to the leading man standard in Hollywood at the time, Johnson slims down his bulky frame and distances himself from professional wrestling and the moniker "The Rock." For the next five years, Johnson appears in mostly family and comedy films that cater to a broad audience and achieve moderate commercial success.

2006

- Johnson stars in *Southland Tales,* a dystopian black comedy thriller. Notably, it's the first film in which he is credited as "Dwayne Johnson" instead of "The

Rock." It's followed by the sports drama *Gridiron Gang,* in which he's credited as "Dwayne 'The Rock' Johnson."

- Johnson founds the Dwayne Johnson ROCK Foundation, an organization that strives to improve the health and self-esteem of at-risk and ill children. Other charitable work Johnson is involved with includes disaster relief with the American Red Cross, pediatric healthcare initiatives such as the Starlight Children's Foundation, Make-A-Wish Foundation, and various educational programs and scholarships.

2007

- Johnson plays the lead role in *The Game Plan,* a Disney family comedy that allows him to live out (fictionally, at least) his frustrated dream of being a professional football player. It is successful commercially and showcases Johnson's comedic skills and ability to carry a movie. It's the last film in which Johnson is credited with his wrestling moniker—moving forward, he'll go solely by "Dwayne Johnson."
- Johnson and Dany Garcia separate amicably, but they remain business partners and close friends. Garcia begins managing Johnson's career in 2008 and has overseen every aspect of his business empire ever since.

2008

- Johnson delivers the induction speech at his father's and grandfather's induction into the WWE Hall of Fame.

- Johnson is cast in the spy action-comedy film *Get Smart*. It's a commercial success, earning $230 million worldwide.
- Johnson finalizes his divorce from Garcia, which is followed by a bout of depression.

2009

- Johnson leads the Disney science-fiction adventure film *Race to Witch Mountain* in which he hopes to bridge his family and action fan bases. It's another commercial success despite not getting great critical reviews.
- Johnson lends his voice to the lead character in the animated film *Planet 51*.

2010

- Johnson has a supporting role in the action comedy *The Other Guys*, as well as the starring role in the film *Faster*.
- After five years of dedication to full-time acting, Johnson recognizes that things are not working as he envisioned. He hasn't managed to make the leap into the top tier of Hollywood stars, and he is feeling distanced from who he is at his core. In a moment of clarity, after the release of *Tooth Fairy*, Johnson decides to change his approach and take a shot at being his authentic self. Johnson, with Dany Garcia by his side as his manager, fires his representation and publicists and surrounds himself with a new team with the same vision as him: going back to what he does best, which is wrestling and action movies. To

this purpose, Johnson returns to the gym to rebuild his muscular physique—he describes his grueling workouts as "anchoring" and "therapeutic"—and moves back to Florida.

2011

- In a pivotal moment in his career that allows him to reconnect with the WWE crowd, Johnson returns to TV on the February 14 edition of *Raw*—after seven years away from wrestling—to announce his role as host of WrestleMania 27, to be held later that year. Additionally, he challenges John Cena, igniting their high-profile rivalry. Johnson and Cena agree to meet for the first time at the following year's WrestleMania.
- Johnson is cast as Luke Hobbs in *Fast Five,* the fifth installment of the *Fast and Furious* movie franchise. The film makes over $620 million in box office revenue. He reprises this role in three sequels and a spinoff, making this role the highest grossing and most successful of his career.

2012

- Johnson and John Cena go head-to-head for the first time at WrestleMania 28, after engaging in notorious taunts and verbal confrontations (including musical battles) that build unprecedented hype for what is advertised as the "Once in a Lifetime" match. Despite being the underdog, Johnson beats Cena in just over thirty minutes. The event breaks the then-record for the most watched and highest-grossing WWE pay-per-view of all time.

- Johnson stars in the family movie *Journey 2: The Mysterious Island.*
- Johnson and Dany Garcia co-found the multi-platform production company Seven Bucks Productions. Seven Bucks Productions has since produced or co-produced most of Johnson's films and TV shows, including *Baywatch* (2017), *Jumanji: Welcome to the Jungle* (2017), *Jungle Cruise* (2021), and *Hobbs & Shaw* (2019). The Seven Bucks banner later expands to include the digital content company Seven Bucks Digital Studios and the advertising agency Seven Bucks Creative.

2013

- Johnson captures his eighth WWE Championship. Shortly after, Johnson challenges John Cena to a rematch of their previous encounter, putting his championship on the line. They battle it out during WrestleMania 29, with Cena coming up victorious this second time around and snatching the championship from Johnson. Johnson suffers brutal injuries from this match and undergoes emergency surgery and extensive rehabilitation.
- Johnson stars in the films *Snitch, G.I. Joe: Retaliation, Pain & Gain, Fast & Furious 6*, and *Empire State.* Combined, these earn $1.3 billion at the box office, making Johnson the top-grossing actor of the year according to *Forbes*.
- Johnson hosts the TNT reality show *The Hero*.

2014

- Johnson plays the title character in *Hercules,* a project he's wanted to develop for many years and a role he felt born to play.
- Johnson hosts and produces another TNT reality series, *Wake Up Call,* in which he helps motivate and empower everyday people facing challenges in their lives.

2015

- Johnson's second daughter, Jasmine—his first child with then-girlfriend, musician Lauren Hashian—is born on December 16.
- *Ballers,* a sports comedy drama TV series with Johnson in the leading role of a retired NFL player, premiers. It runs for five seasons, becoming one of HBO's most successful comedies.
- Johnson stars in the disaster film *San Andreas.*

2016

- Johnson stars in the comedy *Central Intelligence.* The comedic pairing of Johnson and co-star Kevin Hart proves highly successful, and earns them the "BFFs" Kids Choice Award. The movie kickstarts Johnson and Hart's friendship and recurrent partnership in comedy films.
- Johnson voices demigod Maui in Disney's hugely successful animated musical film *Moana,* which earns $644 million at the box office, wins a Grammy, and is Oscar nominated for Best Animated Feature and Best

Original Song. It's a movie close to Johnson's heart: not only does it showcase his Polynesian culture, but the character of Maui is inspired by Johnson's late grandfather "High Chief" Peter Maivia. In *Moana,* Johnson challenges his singing skills with the song "You're Welcome," which ultimately achieves quadruple platinum certification.

- Johnson is named as one of the world's most influential people by *TIME* magazine.
- Johnson partners with athletic apparel company Under Armour to launch Project Rock, a line of footwear, clothing, and other training accessories that has released various collections over the years and which later becomes the official footwear partner of the Ultimate Fighting Championship (UFC).

2017

- Johnson stars in three blockbusters: *The Fate of the Furious, Jumanji: Welcome to the Jungle,* and *Baywatch,* which cement his reputation for rebooting dormant movie franchises (the media refers to him as "franchise Viagra").
- Johnson receives his star on the Hollywood Walk of Fame.
- Johnson receives the award for Entertainer of the Year at the NAACP Image Awards, topping fellow nominees Beyoncé, Regina King, Chance the Rapper, and Viola Davis.

2018

- Action-packed movies *Rampage* and *Skyscraper* fail to reach Johnson's earlier success at the domestic opening weekend box office but prove successful overseas.
- Johnson and Hashian's second child, a baby girl by the name of Tiana, is born on April 17. Johnson frequently flaunts his girl-dad status and close relationship with his young daughters on social media, and he often speaks about women's empowerment.

2019

- Johnson and Lauren Hashian get married on August 18 in a private ceremony in Hawaii.
- Johnson receives the Generation Award at the MTV Movie and TV Awards, which honors actors whose contributions have turned them into household names.
- He also makes the list (as well as the cover) of *TIME*'s 100 Most Influential People annual issue.
- Johnson reprises his role in the sequel *Jumanji: The Next Level.*

2020

- Rocky Johnson dies of a sudden heart attack provoked by a deep vein thrombosis at age 75. A month prior, Johnson and his father fought about inaccuracies in Rocky's 2019 memoir. The two do not reconcile prior to Rocky's death—something Johnson expresses great regret over.

- Venturing into consumer goods, Johnson launches his tequila brand Teremana. The bottom of each bottle is engraved with "TIJASI," a nod to his daughters' names.
- Johnson and Dany Garcia (along with RedBird Capital Partners) purchase the XFL, a professional football minor league founded in 2018 by WWE executive Vince McMahon, with plans to relaunch the league. In late 2023, it's announced that XFL will merge with the United States Football League to become the United Football League (UFL).
- Johnson becomes the most-followed American man on Instagram with more than 200 million followers (and over 300 million followers across all social media platforms).
- During the COVID pandemic, Johnson advocates for health measures such as wearing face masks, social distancing, and coronavirus testing while condemning the politicization of pandemic policies. Johnson collaborates with Under Armour to donate $1 million in the form of personal protective equipment for frontline workers. He also partners with Voss Water to donate thousands of water bottles to first responders during the early stages of the pandemic.

2021

- *Young Rock*, a biographical sitcom produced by Johnson, begins. The series lasts three seasons.
- *Jungle Cruise*, a Disney theme park ride reimagined as a film, is released both in theaters and the streaming platform Disney+ in an innovative hybrid release

strategy due to the ongoing pandemic. Another of Johnson's films, the action-comedy-thriller Netflix original *Red Notice,* becomes the streaming platform's most watched movie of 2021.

- According to a poll, 46 percent of Americans support Johnson's candidacy for president of the United States. In response, Johnson declares his disinterest in pursuing a career in politics—for the time being, at least. He has been a vocal activist of voting rights and endorsed President Joe Biden and Kamala Harris in the 2020 presidential election.
- Johnson launches the energy drink line ZOA Energy.

2022

- After 15 years in the making, Johnson's much-anticipated DC universe superhero film *Black Adam* premiers. As one of the few superhero characters of color, Johnson describes Black Adam as a passion project and the most important role of his career, for which he transforms his body to achieve the best physical shape of his life. Unexpectedly, and despite breaking Johnson's personal record by earning $67 million at the box office during opening weekend and generating $393 million worldwide, the movie's massive budget causes it to fail to break even—crashing Johnson's hopes of building an entire franchise around the character.
- Johnson again lends his voice to an animated character, this time for the *DC League of Super-Pets*.

2023

- In the aftermath of the deadliest fire in the United States in more than a century, Johnson and Oprah Winfrey launch the People's Fund for Maui to help people who had been displaced by the wildfires. They pledge $5 million each and urge others to donate (a request received with some criticism due to Johnson and Winfrey's extensive wealth). Ultimately, the fund gives $60 million to Maui residents.
- Johnson also makes a historic seven-figure donation to the relief fund of the SAG-AFTRA Foundation, which provides financial assistance to the union's members amid the actors' and writers' strikes against major Hollywood studios. It's the single largest donation in the foundation's history.
- Johnson receives the Inspirational Icon Award at The Grio Awards for his continuing support of the Black community.
- Following in his footsteps, Johnson's daughter Simone makes her in-ring WWE debut in 2023 at NXT Stand & Deliver under the moniker "Ava Raine," making history as WWE's first fourth-generation wrestler. Johnson credits wrestling for helping restore their relationship and bringing them closer together after he was absent for most of her childhood due to his hectic career.

2024

- Johnson is appointed to the board of directors of TKO Group Holdings Inc., the parent company of the

WWE and UFC. He also enters into an intellectual property assignment agreement with WWE, under which he gains full ownership of the trademarked wrestling name "The Rock" as well as two dozen other famous nicknames and catchphrases popularized during his wrestling career and are now part of the cultural lexicon—including "The People's Champion," "The Great One," "Know your role and shut your mouth," and "If you smell what The Rock is cooking." Moreover, Johnson obtains property rights to any logos, service marks, costumes, routines, words (such as "jabroni" and "candy ass"), etc., related to his time in the WWE. Not only does this allow Johnson to receive extensive royalty payments in connection to the sale of products bearing his name, but he is now free to take full control of his brand.

- Johnson launches a men's personal care line, Papatui.
- Johnson is back in the ring for the first time in eight years at Wrestlemania 40, during which he competes in the main event match as part of Roman Reigns's tag team in what becomes WWE's highest-grossing event of its history. It's the twelfth WrestleMania match of his career, and the sixth time he headlines it.
- Seven Bucks Productions signs a multi-year, first-look deal with Disney to develop films for theatrical and streaming platforms (with Johnson to potentially star in those projects). The deal also gives the production label the opportunity to collaborate across other Disney divisions.

Acknowledgments

We would like to thank Tobiah Agurkis, Kate Anderson, Henry Begler, Will Carr, John Crema, Marta Evans, Emily Feng, Mira Green, Maeve Hickey, Erin Karasewski, Eve Leupold, Elizabeth Pappas, Erin Rosenberg, Kate Sherman, Lexi Singleton, and Suzanne Sonnier for their invaluable contributions to the preparation of this manuscript.